ALWAYS BE THE SHARK

RECLAIMING YOUR STORY TO RECLAIM YOUR LIFE

STEVIE DAWN CARTER

ALWAYS BE THE SHARK

Carter, Stevie Dawn *Always Be the Shark: Reclaiming Your Story to Reclaim Your Life*

All rights reserved.

Copyright © 2022 by Stevie Dawn Carter

Published by KWE Publishing

Cover art by Michelle Fairbanks

ISBN (paperback):979-8-9852524-0-8 (ebook): 979-8-9852524-1-5

Library of Congress Catalog Number: 2021922588

Dr. Stevie Dawn Carter https://drsteviedawn.com/

KWE Publishing www.kwepub.com

CONTENTS

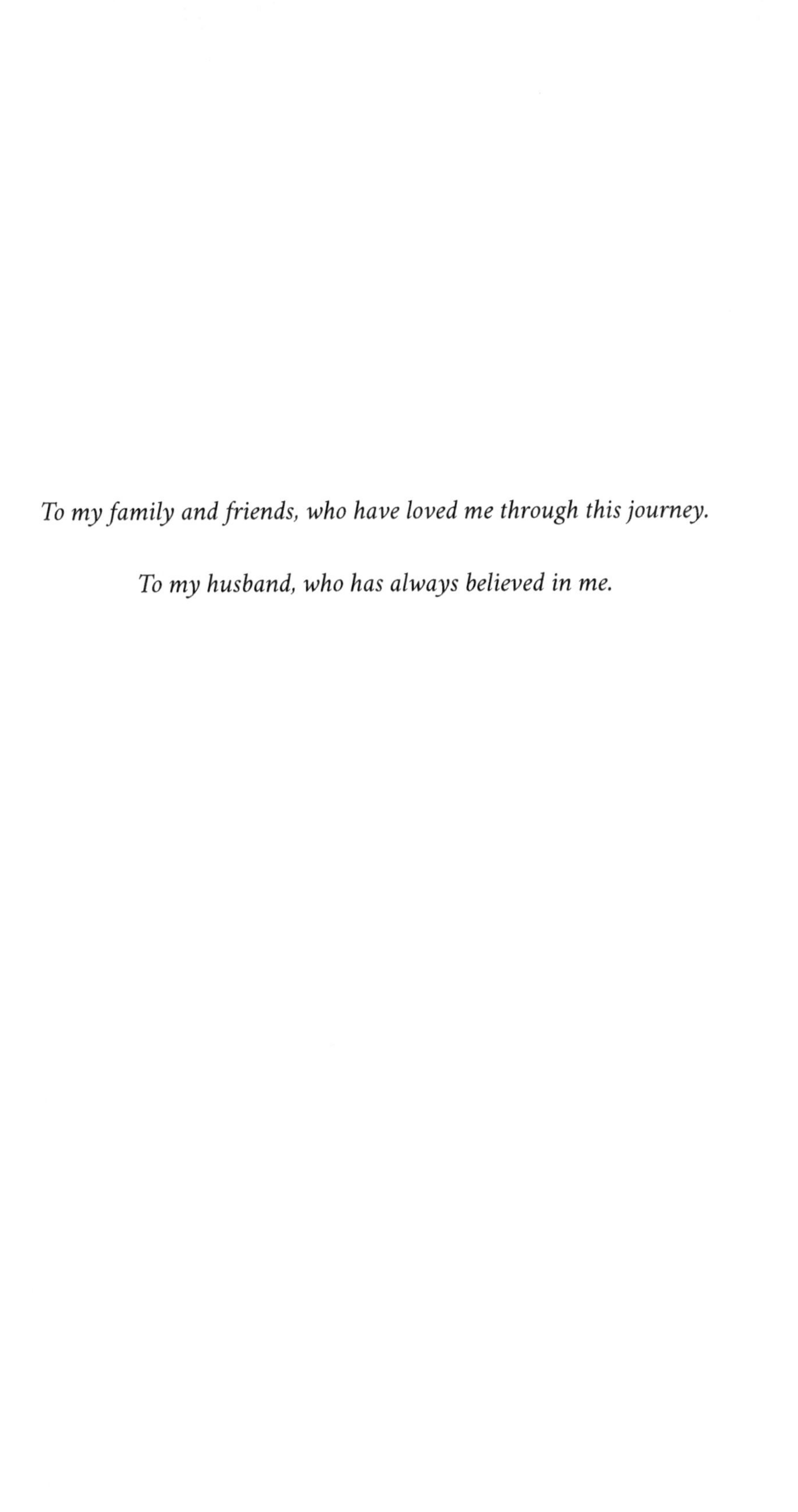

To my family and friends, who have loved me through this journey.

To my husband, who has always believed in me.

ACKNOWLEDGMENTS

While I have always dreamed of putting on a One-Woman-Show, this book is not that. It took an incredible team and tribe to make this book happen and I couldn't have done it without them. Let's start with the team in charge of making this book come to life, not just through words, but through PR, marketing, cover design and all the bits and pieces in between. Thank you to Kim Eley and team for your amazing work in taking my words and making them coherent in a written format. Now, this may seem like a trivial thing to some but I HATE having my picture taken….at least I did, until I met Ariel Peck. She has an incredible gift for not only fabulous photos, like the headshot for this book, but for also making me feel incredibly beautiful in front of the camera. Epicness. Throughout the years of being in business there have been two coaches that have completely changed my trajectory. To my first professional coach ever, Donnie Boivin, thank you for showing me what I was truly capable of when I got out of my own way. I owe you a bottle of rum. And, I really didn't break my bad habits of negative self-talk until Jane M. Powers took me under her wing where I learned how to write a speech and release myself of past guilt and shame. This book would NEVER have happened if two rock stars didn't meet, fall in love and give birth to a rock-star daughter. To Jo Carey and Pete Previte, thank you for being examples of following dreams and leaning fully into the rockstar name. You have always been my biggest cheerleaders no matter how crazy the ideas. And to the stepparents who took me into their families as their own children, thank you to Frank and Deb. You have both supported me which is fantastic, but above that, you both made my parents unbelievably happy, which I treasure. Finally, to my husband, my ride-or-die, my partner in all the things….Matt Carter. I cannot put into words what your support has meant to my life. Just know I love you super bazookas.

*And she lived happily ever after...*it sounds so perfect and romantic and SO unrealistic. While we live in a world where the pressure is to be perfect, it is sometimes difficult to show vulnerability, while still searching for who and what we are, and who we are willing to let the world see.

In her book, *Always Be the Shark: Reclaiming Your Story to Reclaim Your Life*, Stevie Dawn takes you through her own roller-coaster ride and how one conversation with her mom, and one tiny comment from that, changed everything for her. It made me giggle how out of left field those four words were, and yet it will last a lifetime for Stevie Dawn.

As women, we can sometimes—ok most of the time—fine, all of the time—be our own worst critics. We come up with these in-depth scenarios, with cameo appearances by our own kryptonite personas, while appearing on the large screen of our minds in techno-color, that are so real, we are stopped in our tracks. We can't move forward, and we simply stand still, waiting to see the outcome of this recurring nightmare. When we face the reality, they never even happen. If we're lucky, we have someone that will help to wipe the sweat ball we've become, remind us to breathe and take a step forward. Stevie Dawn shows us that all of our head trash is something that we can control and using her six pillars of positive mindset will make the transition that much easier. I'm pretty sure there is a perfect spot on my wall for that giant poster-board reminder.

Throughout our careers as entrepreneurs, corporate executives and volunteers for a cause that is bigger than our dreams, we are all faced with one similar challenge...Am I Enough? Can I really do what is expected of me? Will I fail? What if I succeed? The truth is, navigating this twisty-turvy world is hard. First, it's about stepping out of your comfort zone. Think about it this way, when you step out of your comfort zone, you are going into the unknown. Fear of the unknown can be uncomfortable but sooner rather than later, the unknown becomes the known and that becomes your new comfort zone. It's a tongue twister for sure, but somehow makes sense.

Stepping into this cold place brings up the next reality...Having to do this alone...Why should you have to?

While you have had that power all along to make things happen, Stevie Dawn reminds us once again that it "takes a village" ...and that it's ok to ask for help, as there are women everywhere ready to surround you with their brilliance, their compassion, their love, and that swift nudge when you need it most. Here's what I know...It seems like we are always searching for something...a job, another job, a promotion, a girlfriend, a boyfriend, a husband, a wife, great shoes, someone to listen, someone to trust, great wine, champagne that doesn't cost a fortune, a better tasting protein bar...something. Some of us are searching for that one thing we had when we were little that somehow disappeared or is possibly hiding underneath layers of life. Some of us are searching for that magic bullet to bring value, be relevant, be an influencer, a guru, an expert, a leader. The truth is, it all comes back to mindset.

Being a leader does not mean you are exempt from doubt or fear. You are human, after all. But leaders develop the discipline to manage their concerns and redirect to a grounded, positive mindset.

Every year I come up with a word that means something special to me. This year it was connection. Feeling connected to each other is a basic human need. It's something we've missed, are searching for and is something we all thrive on.

It's a different kind of connection that we want. One that is heartfelt, selfless, and strong. One that we invest in, and others will do the same with us. One that can bring joy, happiness and open doors to things that are more than we thought possible.

Think about who you want to surround yourself with. Who have you been wanting to start a conversation with and who you know will benefit from knowing who you are...? Every year we have 365 opportunities to make the connections that you've been waiting for.

Stevie Dawn and *Always Be the Shark: Reclaiming Your Story to Reclaim Your Life* is that connection you have been searching for. You won't simply flip through it. You will read each and every page, maybe a few times, and write notes in the margins, add post-it notes for those pages you want to come back to again and again and will keep it on your night stand or your desk, or both... and you will know that you are now surrounded by something so amazing, you will want to shout it from the rooftops and make sure everyone you care about will read it and feel the same way.

This is not an ordinary book. It was written by someone who has been there, done that and bought the t-shirt. She is smart, courageous, funny, exciting and is a wonderful friend, an amazing listener and has a thing for sharks.

As I read the book, I laughed, I cried and got goosebumps waiting to hear what my favorite shark would do next. How do you go from wanting to quit to being one of the strongest leaders I know? Simply by following an important philosophy: #always-betheshark.

Moms are usually some of the smartest philosophers around…yours is at the top of the list. Stevie Dawn, you had the choice to give in and give up…you chose to give those words a chance to change your life, and that choice impacted the lives of so many others.

Remember the Old English proverb— *"Just when the caterpillar thought the world was over, it became a butterfly."*

—Judy Hoberman, President, Judy Hoberman and Associates

PREFACE

Based out of Mansfield, Texas, I am a four-time business owner. I have created multi-million dollar success and served the world of business, dance, and art. At seventeen years old, I opened and operated my first dance studio in Australia. I've achieved my doctorate in leadership, where I studied emotional intelligence and leadership development. The best moments of my life include serving in the U.S. Marine Corps, dancing on the Las Vegas Strip, and cage diving with great whites. I'm addicted to sharks, red wine, and coffee, though not necessarily in that order. And I'm the founder of Stevie Dawn Inspires, LLC.

With that bio, you might imagine I've always had a strong, positive mindset, right?

Wrong.

I would be lying if I said that I have always been confident. In fact, I spent years holding myself and my business back because I couldn't shift my mindset. I was too negative, too harsh, and too critical. Not of others, mind you, but of myself.

I wrote this book because I know I'm not alone in feeling this way.

Most people are stuck with underwhelming results because they don't believe in themselves.

Some suffer from strategy overwhelm and can't move forward because they are scared of making a wrong step.

Many are struggling to truly reach unstoppable success because they are noticing all of the "shouldas, couldas, wouldas."

And all of us have the ability to create the lives that we want if we only remove the obstacles and start to see the greatness within.

A shark never swims backwards…it only charges ahead. I invite you to charge ahead with me.

INTRODUCTION

As my heart pounds, I stare straight ahead. Searching. Hoping. Tears start falling down my face.

What is wrong?

"Are you good?" comes the anxious call from outside the bathroom door.

"Be out in a minute," I reply.

Splashing water on my face, running my fingers through my hair, and taking one more long look in the mirror. Plastering on a smile, I walk back to the party.

This can't be right. This can't be the way that life was meant to be. I refuse to accept that this is life for the next however many years I have left to live it. This can't be it. For heaven's sake, it's a party, not an interrogation.

I tell myself that I should be relaxed, that I should hold my head high and feel incredible and successful.

I don't. Instead, I feel like a train wreck.

I would love to say that this meltdown was a one-time occurrence. But that isn't the truth. The truth is that this feeling was happening to me more and more.

I kept expecting <u>her</u> to come back. <u>She</u> was the girl I was back then.

The one who was fearless.

The one who laughed, sang, and danced every day.

The one whose smile wasn't fake.

There wasn't a specific moment or a specific triggering event that took her away from me. Over time, <u>she</u> got pushed out. And now, when I looked in the mirror, I couldn't see her.

I couldn't see myself.

Which begs the question: when did I lose myself?

It wasn't sudden like a gunshot. Losing myself was more like a terrible disease. It took its time. Slowly creeping into the different areas of my life. Dimming my light. Making me quiet, withdrawn, and stuck.

It started in my twenties. Feeling lost and searching for a path. Listening to the "people" of the world telling me to check the boxes.

Get a degree. *Check.*

Get a good job with benefits. *Check.*

Get a husband. *Check.*

Get a house. *Check.*

But all these checked boxes weren't the accomplishments I thought they would be. Looking back, the more boxes I checked, the more "same" I became. Stuck in the boxes that society said were supposed to be "life." Instead of feeling accomplished, I just felt lost. And with every checkbox, my depression mounted.

Then came the panic attacks. The anxiety. Then I put on the mask.

I started wearing a mask in front of others. You know the one. With the pasted-on smile and the response that "Everything is FINE."

I think everyone has that mask. Some of us wear it more frequently than others. For me, over a ten-year span, it began to feel permanent. Like I would never take it off.

But I wasn't always like this.

I used to be fearless. *Not fearful.*

I used to be brazen. *Not shy.*

I used to be happy. *Not sad.*

This mask was smothering me. And I scrounged up my courage and made the decision.

I was going to find that little girl.

The one who believed she could be anything she wanted to be. The one who loved the spotlight. Who used her voice to speak up. Who lived a life filled with fun and adventure. Who was different and embraced those differences rather than hide them under a mask. The girl whose smile lit up a room because her joy was contagious.

That girl was me. **And I was bringing her back.**

There was a time in my life when I shied away from my rockstar name (I was named after the Fleetwood Mac lead singer, Stevie Nicks). When I felt I couldn't own it. I wasn't deserving of it.

Now, in the very marrow of my bones, I knew it was time to own it. It was time to embrace it.

The name.

Myself.

Me.

It was time to BECOME Stevie.

"Living up to her name,
a most magical journey was about to begin."
—from the Christmas Musical, Jingle Jangle, on Netflix

Back in 1999, I found a new passion: West Coast Swing. This slow style of swing dance done to R&B, blues, and pop music was so cool and hip. I loved it! And I got addicted. After taking all of the lessons I possibly could and dancing in many events, I started rising in the ranks on the competitive circuit. Over the years, I had gotten better and better.

Then the inevitable occurred. I stopped winning. I plateaued. I peaked. And if I am being brutally honest, winning was everything to me at that time. And ceasing to win was a problem. At that point, I thought maybe it was time to quit.

One day, while I was on the phone with my mama, the topic of dance came up. I shared with her my plans to give up after my next competition because I felt I just didn't have that "it" factor anymore.

The conversation went like this…

Mama: What do those other dancers have that you don't have?

Me (scoffing): Beauty, grace, youth, flexibility, all the things.

Mama: I don't think that's it.

Me: (rolls eyes)...

Mama: I think the thing they have that you don't have is they're not trying to prove anything. They already know they belong. You just have to go out there and BE THE SHARK.

You know, sharks aren't scared. They aren't trying to prove anything. They're not worried. They know they own their ocean. They keep swimming. They keep being the predator, not the prey. They know they belong. You need to do that in dance.

You just need to be the shark.

Me: Thanks, Mama.

After we hung up, I thought to myself, *What is she on about? Sharks? She must have been watching too many SyFy Channel B-creature movies again.*

I shrugged and laughed. *That's Mama for you*, I thought, and then I went along my merry way.

But that phrase, be the shark, stuck with me.

A few weeks later, at that last dance competition, I was standing backstage about to compete. And I found myself repeating that phrase that Mama shared to myself:

Be the shark, be the shark!

Heck, I even did the hand motion, you know, putting my "fin" on my head with my hands. I did that because I thought that would help me to be the shark!

Well, I went out there on the dance floor, and, I'll tell you, I felt amazing! I had this incredible feeling like I was the only one on the floor. I was up there dancing for the pure joy and fun of it all.

And I won.

In fact, I won the next fourteen events I entered.

For me, confidence is a sense of belonging and that phrase that Mama shared, **be the shark,** was my ticket to that confidence.

I found her again. The me who was fearless.

The me who laughed, sang, and danced every day.

The me whose smile wasn't fake.

I had found that connection between self-confidence and self-awareness.

Becoming Stevie Dawn means always being the shark.

This book is more years in the making than I care to admit. The truth is that I was scared. Scared to write it all out. To share my story, because "who am I" to tell people how to handle their lives and how to find their success? I used to think, *I am just...me.*

However, during the last year, I realized that I was not writing this book for anyone else. I was writing it for me. Gaining clarity on how far I've come. Forgiving myself for the mistakes. Celebrating the small wins.

What follows is the story of my life (well, at least some of it) and the mindset shifts I had to make to truly BECOME myself.

It is the story of losing myself.

Of finding myself.

Of becoming myself.

We all start as ourselves. Then we take this long winding road where we try all the different roles and masks, and then, inevitably we end up coming back to who we were all along. I am not sure that describes everyone, but it definitely fits me.

If this resonates with you, perhaps it is time that <u>you</u> became who you were meant to be.

CHAPTER 1

BECOMING THE CEO (VISION)

SEVERAL YEARS AGO, sitting in my boss's office, she asked me, "So, what's next for you?"

And I froze.

I didn't have an answer. I had no clue what was next for me. I had just earned my Ph.D. The previous five years of my life had been devoted to achieving this big goal and I had achieved it. I had had all these goals I was supposed to achieve and *boom*! I had achieved them. And now, I was lost.

And now what?

I remember it so clearly. Sitting there in my boss's guest chair, thinking, *I have no plan for what's next.*

Have you ever had that kind of feeling after achieving a goal? I know I'm not alone in this. I actually think it happens to all of us. We go after a goal, we focus on the goal, but then once we achieve it, there's the euphoria.

And then there are the inevitable thoughts of, *But what's next? What do I do after this?*

When first hitting their stride with consumers, one of the major television and movie streaming companies aired a commercial introducing something called binge-watching, a new concept at the time. They described binge-watching your favorite show as consuming one after the other without a break, and then, when you're done and no more episodes are left, they said you're in a show hole! A show hole is when you're like, *"Well, what show do I watch next? Like, I've been spending all of this time watching these episodes and now they are over. Yikes, what's next for me?"*

In life, I believe we run into a similar challenge. I call them goal holes. We've set the goals. We have achieved them. And then we're stuck scratching our heads, saying, *"I don't know what to do next!"*

At that moment in my boss's office, my answer to her question about what was next kept reverberating in my brain: *I don't know.* For the life of me, until that moment, I couldn't remember the last time that I didn't know what was next for my life.

What I said was, "Well, I'm just happy to be out of school and I'm just taking it easy."

However, that wasn't the truth. Now, as I sat there, I was uneasy. I had pursued my Ph.D. dream tooth and nail without really thinking about what was going to change, and without asking, *How is this achievement going to impact my life? And why?*

Stunned, I realized the truth: I was chasing it because I was told I was supposed to.

Growing up, there's always a moment when you turn another year older and people ask you, "Do you feel any different?"

"Yes," I always wanted to snarkily say. *"I went to sleep last night and magically when midnight hit, I felt different, older, and super adult-ish, whatever that means!"*

I actually don't believe anything magical happens by turning a year older. But many of us believe something pretty amazing will happen when we achieve a goal. We believe we will be transformed.

As a result, every day, every week, every month, every year we set goals. We set them for small, daily things. It might be a goal to get out of bed earlier, a goal to get to work, or a goal to get a project done by a certain deadline.

We also set big goals: *Where do I want to be in my life in five years?*

Sometimes we set goals and we can't get motivated to achieve them. They seem like good goals, sure, but somehow, we're just not getting it done.

Maybe you've set some goals and then life gets in the way. And now the goal no longer matters. Many of the goals we made in the year 2020, for example, completely changed when the COVID-19 pandemic hit. We set our goals, but then life happened, and the once-important goals no longer mattered.

Sometimes, we do pursue our goals. We focus and bear down and work our butts off. And then, when we finally achieve our goals, we believe we will be transported into a different life. We feel on top of the world!

But how long does that satisfaction and inspiration really last? For most of us, it doesn't last very long. In fact, I remember when I finally achieved that Ph.D. after five long years, I celebrated with a small party with the family. Spent the weekend watching television and eating cake. Then, Monday, I went back to work. Nothing had changed. I had celebrated for three days for something that took my FIVE YEARS to achieve. WOW! You would've thought I could have at least celebrated for a month, right?!

The worst part is when we're laser-focused on a goal, we can actually forget about other important parts of our life. I had ignored my health, my family, and my happiness. But most importantly, I had forgotten why I was even going after this goal in the first place. Sometimes, you forget how the achievement of that goal will really fit into your life. We can become so focused on the goal that we stop asking ourselves if achieving that goal is what's going to make us happy.

Goals Are Great, But Vision Brings Happiness

My client Joan seemed to have it all together. She had the killer job, she had an awesome family—she was set. Yet when she approached me, she was interested in coaching because she felt unmotivated.

She felt stuck. As she described, *"I feel like I am going through the motions of life without really feeling alive."*

Have you ever felt that way? I know I have.

In working together, Joan and I realized that her goals and vision of her life had been established by somebody else. Joan had become dedicated to this specific vision of what her life was supposed to be. What she believed was that she had to have the family, the kids, the job. And she had chased after all of it so hard that she had lost track of what she wanted.

When she reached out to me, instead of Joan's goals, the goals she pursued were for her kids. The goals were for her husband. The goals were the ones that Joan's boss set for her. None of them were truly hers.

No wonder she didn't feel alive.

Working together, Joan and I had to push her outside her comfort zone. When I empowered her to rethink her life in a whole different way, she started making her own goals.

Joan started by painting a vision for her life that she really wanted. Literally, she ended up finding a new hobby, painting. Considering that she picked it up in her forties, she's a remarkable painter.

After gaining clarity, she also changed jobs and entered a new industry that really spoke to her. She's still a great mom, and now that she's chasing her dreams, her kids are inspired. Since she is living for her own goals and not just going through the motions, she is showing up more presently for them, and they have reacted positively toward her change.

What made the difference for Joan? What I've witnessed from watching her and my other amazing clients is that focusing on a goal is helpful, but life is not about the goals. **It's about having a vision for your life.**

Not knowing what the next goal was going to be, not having a plan, was a struggle for me. My "goal hole" dilemma stuck with me. The question I kept asking myself—and later, my clients—was: how do we get past that? And how do we prevent it from happening again?

Having a vision for your life, which is much larger than having a goal, forces you to get out of your rut. Surprisingly, that's what goals can become: ruts and routines that we fall into. Sometimes we don't even realize our goals are keeping us from where we truly want to go.

A vision is the big picture of life. A vision fuels you to get up, jump out of bed, and chase it every single day. A goal is just one area of your life, but your vision includes all of the pieces.

Strategy #1 Picture Your Ideal Life

Right now, I want you to take a minute and think about your ideal life. If I handed you a supercharged magical wand, and with it you could create your best life, what would your new life look like?

Close your eyes. Take a deep breath to clear your mind. Then create the image for yourself in your mind of our best life. Seriously, set down this book for a moment and create your image before you continue reading.

When you have the picture in your mind, I want you to place yourself in the middle of it. Picture every single detail of your ideal life. Think about what you're doing, what you're working on, and who you're with. What are your hobbies? Where do you live? What are you learning? What's your impact?

With that vision fresh in your mind, write it down.
What came up for you?
What did you see in that picture?
Were you in the sun?
Were you in the shade?
Were you inside? Were you outside?
Were you with a family?
Were you by yourself on a mountaintop, were you working with people, or were you working by yourself?

Then I challenge you to ask yourself: how much of that picture is yours? And how much of that picture is something you've been told you're supposed to want?

After this exercise, you may realize you were chasing the dreams and goals that others told you were going to make you happy and successful. You painted them into your vision. Maybe it's about education. Maybe it's about a family. Maybe it's about having children. Maybe it's about having a certain type of job working in an office.

You see, throughout our life, those boxes, like check boxes on a form, are set out for us by society, by our parents, by our teachers, and by our communities. And it's not all negative. It's often a good thing. We need some modeling to create our vision.

At a certain point in time, however, we need to pick up the paintbrush and paint our own vision. It can't be about what others tell us to do or to value. It has to be about what we want, and what is going to make us have a fulfilled, beautiful life.

When our goals are set by others, it's really easy to lose sight of that vision because it's not ours; we don't own it. It is hard to get out of your box and create your new box. It takes a lot to really push outside those comfort zones, to start looking at reprogramming your mind, to start focusing on the things you want, not just the things that you were told to want. The truth is that we think if we check those boxes, success is going to be a straight line. But success is *never* a straight line. It's a messed-up scenic journey, filled with failures and roundabouts and U-turns.

CEOs and Employees

As I was going through this journey, trying to figure out my next step after being stumped by my boss's question, I realized that the vision that had been painted for me was not mine. Then, I knew that I needed to figure out a way to pick up the paintbrush and paint it myself, write my own story, and create my own future based on what I wanted out of life.

Wanting to make a change, I found a coach who took me through the process, the journey, of learning how to think differently and learning how to create my own vision. I wish I could say it just came naturally.

It didn't. Initially, I struggled to embrace it. I had been programmed to think in the same way for so long that it felt like my own brain was fighting me.

I then decided to do the type of research that would lead me to the goal of achieving my Ph.D. I dove into research and what I discovered is that there are two kinds of people: there are CEOs and there are their employees.

These are not just job titles.

CEOs or chief executive officers make decisions for the betterment of their entire company. They spend their days bouncing back and forth through meetings and activities because of all the different departments they oversee. They have to make sure that the financial department is talking to the sales department, and so forth.

A CEO executes decisions confidently because they have the vision. And the most effective CEOs are the ones who are able to talk about the vision, where they're going, paint the picture for everyone, and motivate people to make it happen.

Employees make decisions based on their lanes, their directions, their paths in the sandbox, mostly because of what their boss tells them to do. They spend most of their day in their own departments. As a result, they're siloed. They don't get to see all the other departments, how their work fits into the whole company, and how their work impacts other employees. They often lack the confidence they want because they don't know what the outcome is going to be.

I realized that I must be the CEO of my life and not the employee. I vowed to treat my life like a company. It might sound funny for one person to be a company. However, when you look at it, a company has lots of different parts. And we as people have lots of parts as well. I need to make decisions that are about the whole me, that would get me to where I wanted to go, to have a vision of where that is and what I'm chasing. I want to spend my day bouncing back and forth from section to section and not just spend it in one lane.

I'm not saying that you have to start your own company or become an entrepreneur. What I'm saying is that you need to be the CEO of your life.

When you are the CEO of your life, you are in the driver's seat and you take control. You get to make decisions that are aligned with your vision of success. You paint the picture of what you want your life to look like. And then, you chase opportunities that will get you there. You are the one to make it happen.

After my conversation in my boss's office, it struck me: *this is where I am missing out.* I wasn't the boss of my life. I was still letting society, my parents, my mentors, and other people guide me because I wasn't even sure where I wanted to go.

I was still stuck in that goal hole.

Strategy #2 Write Down Questions

I'm not a big journal fan, but I love to write down questions because they make me think. To empower myself, I started writing down questions in my journal.

- How am I performing as a CEO?
- Am I making decisions?
- Am I running my life?
- How is each department of my life?
- Am I good with my health?
- Am I good with my finances?
- Am I good with my job?
- Am I good with my relationships?
- Am I making decisions that are about all of those aspects of my life?
- Am I learning?
- Am I growing?
- Am I being innovative?
- Am I doing those things that all great CEOs do, talking about my vision and painting a picture of my vision?
- Am I motivating myself to get there?

As I started asking myself these questions, I realized I needed to make changes.

I'm going to be really candid here: It seems that we're trained from a very young age to think like employees. As kids, our parents tell us the path and then our teachers tell us the path, and then society and cultural pressure tell us the path. And we follow it. At a certain point, we have to become the boss. We have to become the leader. It's not easy at all. I know for me, #adultingishard.

When you've gone from thinking like an employee to adopting a CEO mindset, and you've made the shift to adulting, there's no course or class on how to do this. We often get stuck in a rut. Let's face it, it's easier to do what we've always done than try to figure out how to be the boss of our own lives.

You might be thinking, *Yeah, Stevie Dawn, this is great, but I don't know how to create a vision for my life.* You might be wondering how to set goals for yourself, and wondering how to balance this idea of being the boss and having a vision and still working for a company where you do have a boss. You may be thinking, *This is really overwhelming.*

It's okay to feel this way. After all, this is a new idea.

Trust me, now that you have this idea, you're going to be thinking about it all the time. It's going to totally change the way you approach your life, which is awesome.

Strategy #3 Create a Vision Checklist

Let's start by making a yes or no list. We're going to create a vision checklist and use it to confidently execute on opportunities. Take out a sheet of paper, and draw a line down the middle. Write "Yes" on one side and "No" on the other. As you go through your day, think about what decisions you are making. I want you to start recording what you're saying yes and no to.

As you write your items in the "yes" and "no" columns, realize for everything you put on the "yes" column, you're saying "no" to something else. At the end of the week, ask yourself, where do you need to make a change? Where did you say "yes" when you should have said "no"?

For example, let's say it is the end of the day, and your boss says, "Hey, I need volunteers to work this weekend." What is the impact of making this decision? On the one hand, if you say "yes" to your boss, it could be good for your career. You could get in the good graces of the boss, right? But what are you saying "no" to by sacrificing your weekend? Self-care, family time, church service, right? For everything we say "yes" to, we're saying "no" to something else.

Be cognizant of these decisions. Own the fact that you are making them. I don't want you to feel like those decisions are being made for you because—guess what?—they aren't anymore. Start tracking it so you can tackle it.

When I did this exercise for myself, I realized that I was saying "yes" to a lot of work demands for many years, which meant I was saying "no" to a lot of family time. Nowadays, I may have gone too far the other way. I notice that I say "yes" to all the family time and "no" to many work opportunities. Here's the truth: It's never a 50/50 balance. But once I started tracking my decisions, it was easier to tackle which ones I needed to change.

Strategy #4 Examine Your Vision

Next, let's go back to that activity we did at the very beginning of this chapter where you envisioned your life. Look at what you wrote down as you were imagining your ideal life.

- What are the things that show up?
- What are your personal values, the things you value, and the things you want to have?
- What do you want to make sure you do?

When you start examining what's in your vision, you will be able to choose the activities and opportunities that get you where you want to be. It could be happiness. It could be time with family. It could be more time at church or in service. It could be all kinds of things.

Strategy #5 Make Your Vision Stick With Your List

Next, pick three or four of these things from your vision of your ideal life and write them on a sticky note. Please place this sticky note where you can see it frequently. Maybe it is on your bathroom mirror. Perhaps it will live on your computer monitor where you work, or in your car so you see it whenever you drive. Make it super visible so it always catches your attention. This is your new checklist. This is your checklist that is just for you.

Your checklist will change over time. As you accomplish things, you'll mark them off the list and you'll put in new things that are part of your vision. As a result, your vision will keep getting clearer. Since our vision can change, this is not a forever list. That's why I encourage you to write your list on a sticky note so you can easily tear it off and rewrite it anytime you need to.

As an example, I want to share my current list of four things with you and what I do to realize my vision.

1. Joy

Joy is a big part of my life. When I picture my ideal life, I envision it with a smile from ear to ear, where I am beaming because I'm so happy.

Since joy is really important to me, I'm making decisions as CEO of my life that are going to fill me with joy. When an opportunity comes across my desk, I ask myself, *"Is it going to lead me to feel joyful?"* If it's not, it is not worth doing. Asking myself this question is a decision-making tool. I use it to decide if something's aligned or not.

2. $ Freedom

My second vision is freedom with a dollar sign, which represents financial freedom. I know what my financial freedom number is. It is the amount of money I want to make in order to feel financially free. By the way, if you haven't thought about that financial number for yourself, please do. It's very empowering to figure out. So, I know what my financial freedom number is.

Since I have a sticky note with the number on it, I use it as another decision-making tool. Every time I have to make a decision about an opportunity, whether to spend money on vacation, whether to spend money on this investment, whether to invest more in my business, whether to say yes to this client, all of those questions, I look at that number on my sticky note and ask myself, "Is it aligned with that number? Is it getting me closer to that number?"

3. Stage(s)

I love speaking and coaching. When I envision my life, I am on a really big stage. That's what I see in my vision for my life. So anything that gets me closer to that stage, that moment with my audience and my clients, I'm doing it.

4. Connection

Over the years, connection has become more and more important to me. I used to be a solo act when I was single and all by myself. But my vision has changed. And now my vision involves my family, my friends, and my clients. I want to have deep connections with all of the people in my life.

I have realized I'm not okay with acquaintances. I want friends, I want "ride-or-die" people in my life. Since I'm going to focus on connection, it means I will devote time and effort to those people in my life.

With every decision I make, it must meet up with all four of the priorities on my sticky note. If a specific choice would get me closer to #2, my financial freedom number, but will not bring me closer to #1, my joy, it's not enough. **The outcome of my decision has to**

include all of these things in order for me to say yes to it, which goes right back to that initial "yes" or "no" list.

What are the things you value in your vision? What are some things you want to say "yes" to? When you make your list on a sticky note, trust me, you're going to start choosing things because of it. You start realizing what you're saying "yes" to. And if you're going to say "yes," you will ask yourself, W*ill the outcome be aligned to my vision? Is this a decision that I should make for the betterment of my whole life?* This decision-making process really, really helps you realize your vision.

Who Is the Real CEO?

Finally, I challenge you to think differently about the idea of a CEO. When I was going through this process, I was struggling with the title. Candidly, to me, CEOs were stuffy, older, rich people who owned huge multi-bazillion dollar companies. Those were CEOs. I struggled with calling myself a CEO as I didn't see myself that way.

Strategy #6 Retitle Yourself

As I was working with my coach, she said, "Let's retitle it. It's not 'chief executive officer.' It's 'confidently executing on opportunities.'"

That sounds cool! Now I say I am the CEO because I do want to confidently execute on the opportunities given to me. And I love telling my clients that they're the CEO of their lives.

Remember that at the end of the day, the relationship you have with yourself is the most important relationship of your life. Are you the boss? Are you taking ownership? Are you driving that ship, that boat, that car, whatever you want to call it? Are you taking control of your journey?

How are you painting a vision with the paintbrush? Decide not to let anybody else tell you what's going to make you happy, what you should be chasing, but instead choose that for yourself. You are the most important relationship you will ever have. And you owe it to yourself to be the CEO. You owe it to yourself to be the leader.

Checklist for becoming the CEO

- Recognize when you're in a goal hole
- Picture your ideal life
- Write down questions
- Create a vision checklist
- Examine your vision
- Make your vision stick with your list
- Retitle yourself as the CEO

CHAPTER 2

THE CYCLES OF LIFE

ONCE I MADE the decision to finally become the CEO of my life, I knew in my soul where I had to start.

At the beginning.

> *"Let's start at the very beginning,*
> *a very good place to start..."*

This is Julie Andrews' famous line from *The Sound of Music*.

By the way, you should probably know right now that I love music, just the way you would assume with me being named after the famous musician Stevie Nicks. Be prepared as there will be many musical quotes in this book.

If you take a snapshot of where you are right now—what is happening or not happening in your life—it can all be traced back to the beginning. What happened to us as children. The thoughts we explored, the ideas we were exposed to, the experiences we had with others. These all shape us through the years. In a way, our childhood made us who we are as adults. Some people rebel against their upbringings. Others toe the line. It all comes together to make us the person we are. Which leads to the very existential question: Who are you?

But I digress.

As I started on my journey to "Becoming Stevie" (yes, I called it that and wrote the title in my journal), I knew I had to take a look at the thoughts and ideas that I had back then to see where I had gone astray.

What I know is that mindset is everything. Our thoughts lead to our actions. Therefore, if we can change our thoughts, we can change our life. And at that point, I realized my life needed some changes. I went back through my thoughts and I made a list of the ones I had back then and the ones that I had now. Thoughts about myself…

Then	Now
I can do anything.	I am a good teacher.
I am special.	I am average.
I am a high achiever.	I am neurotic, overwhelmed, depressed.
I am smart.	I am the dumbest person in my class.
I am a dancer.	I am a person who used to dance.

WOW. What a difference. No wonder I was unhappy with these negative thoughts. And these were just some of the thoughts swirling around my brain. My "now" list, in fact, was a lot longer, and included:

- I am unworthy.
- I am not good at marriage.
- I am a burden.

You get the picture. When did I become so filled with self-hatred? I mean, that's what it was. I was hating myself, and as I started really processing through each thought, I realized that there really wasn't a reason.

These thoughts had changed over years and years through a variety of different experiences. That boy who cheated on me in high school. Being told I was slow in school. Not getting a part I auditioned for. Washing out of the Marine Corps. Having my first marriage end in divorce in less than two years.

All of these MOMENTS had rewired my brain and changed these thoughts. The thoughts that were plaguing me in my 30s had been there for years and I wasn't even aware of it.

Awareness Is Critical to Success

Strategy #7: Adopt the Success Model (BEBO)

We must become aware of our thoughts, for it is our thoughts that dictate our results. Back in my school days, I had come across a development model made famous by Brooke Castillo, called the Self-Coaching Model. This model stated that your thoughts control your outcomes. Through my education in emotional intelligence and leadership, I adapted the model into my own Success Model.

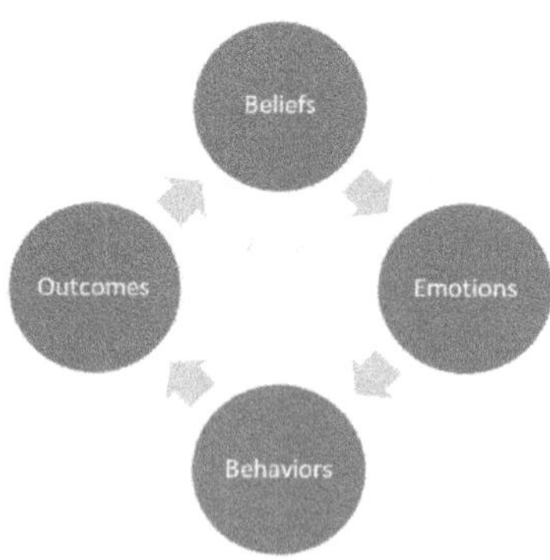

Your **B**eliefs activate your Emotions.
Your **E**motions influence your Behaviors.
Your **B**ehaviors dictate your Outcomes.
Your **O**utcomes Prove Your Beliefs.

I call it BEBO (think of it like the sound a fun robot would make). BEBO is how I truly learned to change my life as I finally understood why I was stuck and unhappy. BEBO is a cycle and it can be vicious or victorious depending on your thoughts.

For example, let's say that you stand in front of the mirror and the thoughts start swirling. Thoughts such as *I am too fat. I really need to lose weight. I wish this shirt would fit better.* These beliefs activate emotions like shame, fear, guilt. Which leads me to....well, when I don't feel my best, I eat ice cream. I mean, isn't that the best option? So I eat the ice cream, which means I will show up the same size (if not bigger) tomorrow. My outcome then proves my original belief...I am fat.

This is a vicious cycle.

Let's look at another example.

You have applied for a promotion. You wake up the morning of the interview and you start thinking, *I am never gonna get this. I don't have the experience they are looking for. Bob has never liked my work and he's on the panel.* These thoughts activate emotions such as fear, insecurity, anxiety. Those emotions influence you to get super nervous, to fidget, and not to give a good interview. A bad interview means you don't get the job, which proves the belief...you weren't gonna get it.

Vicious, right?!

It really is incredible how much our thoughts can dictate everything in our lives, which is why we have to become aware. Not just aware, but critically aware. We must be relentless in examining the beliefs that swarm through our brains and in deciding which beliefs are serving us and which beliefs are not.

On my journey, I learned that a lot of my thoughts were keeping me stuck. I didn't need my knowledge. I didn't need more money. I didn't need a man! I simply needed to take control. Control over my beliefs. That's it.

Easy to say but hard to do.

Several years ago, I was feeling pretty great about life. I had married the true love of my life, my best friend, Matt. We had started this side hustle business in corporate training, and I had obtained my Ph.D. I had my whole life ahead of me.

And yet, something was missing.

I had been in the world of academia for over twelve years. Since going back to school to obtain my master's degree, I had been constantly teaching in the college classroom or supporting students through co-curricular activities.

Honestly, even getting my Ph.D. had been a decision made because I wanted to become the president of a college. However, by the time I had obtained the degree and done my research, I was burned out. I wasn't sure that higher education was the right fit for me. I just wanted something different.

So, my newlywed husband and I started a corporate training company under the name Stevie Dawn Inspires, LLC. The goal was to take the teaching element of being in the classroom that I enjoyed and bring it to the corporate world. Basically, our company would allow me to teach in a different environment.

It was a great idea and I loved the concept. Matt gave me the gift of time. He said that he would keep his job and support us while I chased my dream (he truly is a prince), and so I quit. I had one corporate client and no real plan, but I gave my notice anyway and left the professional world that I had known. It all seemed so exciting that first year. Sure, I had doubts. Yep, I definitely got scared. But it was gonna be okay. I had time to figure it out. I was great in the classroom and I had run a business before. So I could totally do this. *I got this!* That's what I kept telling myself, anyway.

My beliefs were solid.

Or so I thought.

Then, after months of enjoying the yoga pants, no-makeup lifestyle and hanging behind a computer screen, I realized that I was gonna have to get out there and do something. I was going to have to find clients. I was going to have to sell. And that's when things started to slip. I had meeting after meeting and nobody bought. Everyone thought the idea of teaching emotional intelligence to corporate leaders was a good one. Yet, I couldn't seem to make money.

I had some early success, but I gave so many discounts that I was working for minimum wage. That is not my idea of successful entrepreneurship. I wanted to make millions. Actually, back then, I would have settled for making tens of thousands in a given year. It just wasn't working. And the vicious cycle started...I believed they weren't going to buy. That made me feel desperate. Desperation made me nervous, and I lacked confidence in the conversation, which meant they didn't buy. The cycle kept repeating itself.

Then, my coach at the time helped me to learn a concept called Equal Business Stature. This idea says that if you go into a meeting believing that you are equals, then everything will flow more naturally and sales will happen easily. So I tried it. Before my meetings, I would sit in my car or at my computer and repeat the following to myself:

I am the CEO of a company, just as they are.

I am successful, just as they are.

I care about my team, just as they do.

I repeated it at least three times before going into the meeting or picking up the phone. And the change wasn't immediate. But over time, the conversations became more confident. I stopped acting out of desperation. I stopped giving discounts. And my revenue increased. By a lot. I went from making $17,000 one year to making $158,000 the next.

Now, that is a victorious cycle.

Shifting my beliefs about myself shifted my outcomes. In fact, this was the start of a true turning point in my life, and within a few years, I had enabled my husband to leave his corporate grind, I hired a team, and we were living the happiest of lives...for a while, but that's a different story.

The point is that a small change in belief can create BIG results. You just have to stop the vicious cycle and change it to a victorious one.

So, how do you change beliefs? We are each different, and certain techniques that work for some don't work for others. Therefore, I will be sharing a variety of strategies and tactics throughout this book. Try each one and see which seems to help you the most.

Strategy #8 Shine a Light on Your Beliefs

This strategy to make your success cycle victorious is what I also call Retracing. As you've seen from my story, there are a lot of hidden beliefs, ideas, and thoughts that grow in us over the years. Retracing is about shining a light on them.

Take out a sheet of paper and start listing all of your accomplishments. Think of it as a timeline of your life. Start as far back as you can remember and list every single thing you achieved. From winning a softball game, to learning to ride a bike, to successfully graduating high school, and so on. Anything that you achieved, accomplished, or completed can make the list. Try to think of as many as you can. There are no right or wrong answers here. This is you celebrating yourself.

Once you have all that goodness written down, let's take it one step further. For each accomplishment, write a statement of a belief that you had about yourself in that moment. Try to think back. How did it feel when you rode that bike? What did it feel like when you got your degree? Write down those beliefs. What did you think about yourself then? What do you think about that experience now? Are the beliefs different?

For example, maybe then you thought riding a bike was so tough and when you achieved it you felt unstoppable, with the wind whipping through your hair as you rode down the block. Now, your thought is, *Well, that was just a bike. And then I promptly fell off and skinned my knee*. How our beliefs have changed.

Highlight those positive beliefs. Scratch out the negative ones.

Realize that you are still unstoppable, skinned knee or not.

Realize that you are capable of love, even if you have been divorced.

The goal of Retracing is to find those positive beliefs from the past and bring them into the present. Write these new beliefs for yourself and start shifting into a victorious cycle.

- Read them daily.
- Pray over them.
- Meditate with them.
- Allow the past to become present.

Emotions, Behaviors, and Outcomes

Strategy #9 Tracking Your Emotions for the Win

How do you track your emotions? One of the best strategies is becoming aware of what's happening in your life when emotions hit you. Knowing what triggers you helps you better understand what you're getting emotional about.

I mean, I don't know about you but I'm that person who starts to cry the minute the ASPCA commercial comes on TV with the dogs. Why? It's because I love animals, and the music in these commercials pulls at my heartstrings. The reason this impacts me is because I am a super empathetic person.

What about you? What emotions do you feel in certain situations, and what can you learn about yourself by identifying them? One of the easiest ways to track your emotions is to carry a little notebook or track it in your phone. Every time you feel an emotion throughout the day, jot it down, whether you're writing down the word "stress", "excitement", "sadness" or "anger". Many of my clients carry a little notebook in their purse, and every time they're feeling something, they just jot it down. Make sure to capture the details, including the place, the location, the time, the date, the people around you, the environment, the music, and the temperature of the air.

It's really hard to work on our beliefs when we're not tracking the emotions that we feel. When you can identify your emotions, each and every day, you can start to work backwards using the success model to figure out where those emotions came from. You can trace it back to a specific belief that activated those hormones that activated that emotion.

Get in the habit yourself. Write down everything you can about that moment while you are experiencing that emotion, and then you can start to look for patterns for those triggers so that you can better handle your emotional strength.

Strategy #10 Investigate your Habits

Let's talk about a strategy for behaviors. Often I use the words "behavior" and "habit" interchangeably. The reason I do this is because the behaviors we repeat over and over again are our habits. One of the easiest ways to see the success model in action is to really investigate your habits.

Take a look at the things you do every single day. Just as you track your emotions, start by tracking your behaviors. Record the time when you get up in the morning. How many cans of Diet Coke you are drinking, or how many times you refill at the coffee pot? When are you feeling good, and when are you feeling bad? How many times do you open your email during the day? How many times do you scroll through Facebook?

After you've kept track for a few weeks, start looking at the habits you do every day. Identify which of these habits are serving you and which are not. And once we can identify the habits that are good for us, do more of the good habits, and stop doing the bad ones.

Using the habits as a starting point, you can work backwards. Which emotions make you feel like those habits are the right thing to do? From those emotions, what are the mental triggers that cause those emotions to happen? We can trace our habits back to our beliefs; we just have to work backwards. It all starts with tracking those habits so we can develop a strategy around our outcomes.

Strategy #11 Tell Me What You Want, What You Really Really Want (A Spice Girls' Song)

Do you know what outcome you really want? It's okay if you aren't sure. When we first start working together, many of my clients have no clue what they want. When I ask them, "what do you want for your life, what is your vision," they can't come up with anything. If we don't know what outcomes we're actually searching for, how do we know if we are reaching for them or not?

Now is the time to think about your outcome and record it. Start by taking a sheet of paper and write down three things you would like to have happen in the next 60 days. Take five minutes to identify which three things would push you towards your life goals. Next work backwards from those outcomes. Which habits and behaviors would you need to have in order to achieve your goals? How would you need to feel, to make these outcomes happen? What beliefs do you have to have in order to see those outcomes through?

We have to know what our outcomes are so that we can plan a strategy from our beliefs to our emotions to our behaviors that makes the outcome inevitable. Success is always unstoppable.

There you have it...the Success Model in action. Keep this model in mind as we proceed as we'll refer back to it throughout this book.

Checklist for the cycles of life

- Adopt the Success Model (BEBO)
- Shine a light on your beliefs
- Track your emotions
- Investigate your habits
- Know what you really want

CHAPTER 3

THE SIX PILLARS OF UNSTOPPABLE SUCCESS

"Don't tell me there's too far to go.
I know that I'm unstoppable.
I'm ready now.
Nothing's gonna slow me down.
'Cause finally I see."
—Journey,
From "Square Root of Possible," Jingle Jangle: A Christmas Journey

I WOULD LOVE to say that the journey to Becoming Stevie was an easy one. A direct path. A straight line. We all know that's not the way life works, though. The journey is ongoing. Our journey as individuals will never be completed as we continue to grow and change until the end of our lives. So, I have had to accept one of the hardest lessons in life…

There is no destination. It is the journey we must enjoy.

When I came across this phrase, "unstoppable success," it stayed with me. The words just made sense to me. That success is not a destination, yet a series of places where we check boxes and celebrate. That as we move forward in our lives, we are unstoppable. There is no one force that can halt our success except ourselves.

When I was working on becoming a professional speaker, one of the biggest hurdles I faced was convincing myself that I was worthy. See, every book, course, and training out there tells you that to be a highly sought after speaker, you have to share your story. I had seen so many speakers over the years with incredible stories to share. They had overcome obstacles such as homelessness, severe injury, trauma, and more. Me? I was just an average, white middle-class woman who wanted to change the world. I didn't have a story. Who was I to stand and speak about being unstoppable? What had I overcome?

It was then that I realized...I had overcome the obstacle that everyone everywhere faces: myself.

See, this is our truly shared obstacle. Regardless of financial or physical limitations, all of us face the obstacle of our own minds, our own thoughts and beliefs. So why wouldn't I share that story? Because it was clearer to me than anything I had ever spoken about. While I studied a wide range of topics during my tenure in academia and conducted training sessions across the country, the one topic that stood out was that we are ALL unstoppable...if we can get out of our own way. We are the obstacle to overcome, and all of us, every single person deals with it.

Some of us are just bigger obstacles than others (LOL).

So, I stood up and started speaking out. Sharing my story of comparison, mindset blocks, and deep depression. I talked about those boxes I tried to fit in and then busted out of. I talked about my need to believe in myself more than I ever thought possible. In starting to share these stories, I realized the steps along my journey. This BECOMING technique involves 6 key pillars, each of which have been an area of difficulty for each of my clients. Just as I did. These became my pillars. These became my daily reminders of what we must learn, know, and internalize in order to truly be unstoppable.

Bold Confidence
Elevated Habits
Captivating Vision
Opportunity-Focused
Magnetic Mindset
Emotional Resilience

I have dedicated one chapter of this book to each of these powerful pillars. Through these pillars, you will see examples of how each pillar shaped my own life and the lives of others. You will also have access to strategies that will help you to implement these pillars into your own life to truly become who you are meant to be.

Before we dive in deep, I think it is helpful to see the big picture of how these pillars create the foundation for unstoppable success.

Bold Confidence
Bold confidence is the pillar that takes the most cultivation because confidence is something that comes and goes throughout our lives. We have experiences that build our confidence and we encounter situations that cut it off at the knees. Confidence impacts everything around us. Our relationships (personally and professionally), our ability to close clients, win deals, or gain a promotion. Confidence impacts our abilities to speak up in difficult situations. Deal with our families during the holidays, and answer the phone when telemarketers call. Everything comes down to confidence and knowing where to find it and how to grow it are some of the most impactful skills one can possess.

Elevated Habits

Habits control our lives. The good ones and especially the bad ones. We are what we habitually do, and therefore, gaining awareness of and confidence in our habits can really move the needle in our lives. I was never a big believer in habits until I became a business owner. It was then that I discovered habits are important, and that they can make or break ya, both in the professional and personal sphere. It is our habits in our thinking and our everyday interactions that allow us to truly embrace who we are. Elevated habits lead to elevated results and create true growth and joy in our lives.

Captivating Vision

For years, I lived my life according to someone else's plan. Their roadmap. Never stopping to consider if that was the direction, I truly wanted to go. In order to truly live a life that is YOURS, you must be able to see what you want. Not just a goal, but a captivating vision for the life you want to have. When your vision is so compelling and so aligned with your soul that you cannot help but to take a step towards it...that is when success becomes within reach. We often allow our vision to be hijacked by others' ideals or our comparison of ourselves to them. Unstoppable success comes from being able to keep your eye on the prize, so let's make it pretty.

Opportunity-Focused

Have you ever been called a pessimist? The truth is that we all have bad days, and sometimes we are going to only see the negative outcomes. But to step into our power, to become who we are meant to be, we have to focus on the opportunities over the obstacles. Over the years, I had become fearful. No longer taking risks or putting myself out there because I was scared of failure. What I learned is that when you become opportunity-focused, you take steps towards opportunities just to see where they go. Knowing that they may not work out but that the journey is much more impor-tant than the destination.

Magnetic Mindset

For years, I thought the law of attraction, affirmations, and positive thinking was just woo-woo nonsense. That those types of things couldn't really work. Yet, as I allowed myself to focus on mindset and my beliefs, as the success model started to take shape in my life, it became clear that those woo-woo things are for reals! Using a magnetic mindset, you can design and create the life that you want. You can make the things you imagine become reality. You can change the world.

Emotional Resilience

Emotional resilience is one of my favorite topics to talk about...like, ever. Because I feel that our emotions hold us back from so many great experiences simply because we let them control all facets of our life. However, if we can learn how to become aware of our emotions and how to use them to bounce back from tough situations, we are unstoppable.

Before we dive into the first pillar, I want you to take a moment and consider the thoughts going through your head.

Which of these pillars have you already thrown out as "never gonna work for me"? Which of these pillars do you already feel are your strengths? Which pillars do you want to avoid?

Inevitably, when I share these six pillars from the stage during a presentation, I see body language change in some participants. Arms start to cross. People start to pick up their phones. They have already decided that one or more of these are not going to work for them. So, here is my request...keep an open mind and open heart to these ideas.

I didn't believe in them all either when I first started, but I learned over time that they work.

For me.

For my clients.

For you.

Just take a breath and allow yourself to be open to the ideas. You just might surprise yourself.

CHAPTER 4

BOLD CONFIDENCE

I WANT you to think about a time in your life when you felt super confident, like you legit felt you were going to crush it.

I want you to think back on one of those moments. Maybe it's from work. Maybe it's something in your personal life. Maybe you're thinking back to childhood. Maybe it was when you won the third-grade spelling bee. I want you to think about a time when you felt super-duper confident.

Savor it for a moment. Remember what it felt like. It was such a good moment.

I want you to give us the other words that go with that feeling because here's the thing. Confidence is pretty vague, and it's a pretty big idea, but confidence makes most of us feel other emotions, too.

Maybe it's excitement.

Maybe it's feeling capable.

Maybe it's feeling competent, calm and peaceful.

What other feelings do you feel besides just confidence?

You see, confidence is different for every person. And so, if we're really going to tackle our own confidence, we have to know what kind of feelings come up for us when it comes time to be confident.

How do you feel? Are you a creative butterfly, proud, ready for anything? Some words that my clients have used to describe their feelings of confidence are:

Abundant, accepted, smart, proud, good, happy, energized, competent, intelligent, exhilarated.

These are great words. For me, confidence is all about belonging. When I know that I'm in the right place at the right time with the right mojo, that's when I feel the most confident. That's what confidence is for me. It's a sense of belonging.

Now, this is less fun to do, but I want you to think about a time when you weren't so confident. Think about a time maybe where you lost that confidence.

Sometimes, when we think about losing our confidence, we think about public speaking, conversations, and interactions. But I think the number one place where we lose confidence is in our decision-making. We've all made decisions that we look back on and say, "Well, that wasn't a great decision."

One of the times when I lost my confidence the most was after my marriage went bad. You know, how do you get back up on the metaphorical horse? That's what everyone tells you to do when a relationship fails. You know what no one tells you? No one tells you how exactly to get back into a relationship when your last relationship didn't work out well.

I started doubting my ability to make decisions, my ability to trust myself. Even when I found the amazing man who would become my husband, I doubted myself. I wasn't confident. I don't mean I wasn't confident with him or with putting myself out there on the dating scene. No. I lacked basic confidence. I kept asking myself, But what if this goes bad? What if I'm not cut out for this?

To recapture my confidence meant that I had to remember what it felt like to belong in my own skin. Before the relationship fizzled, I remembered feeling like I was in the right place at the right time with the right mojo. That made me confident. So while other people around me would see it as I was before, a bold, confident person, I saw it myself as *I'm just where I belong.* I felt a sense of belonging in that moment. So today, that's what we're going to get for you. We want to unlock your bold confidence so that you can be the shark in your own life.

Anyone can go through the motions and live their lives according to what they've been told to do by their family, their friends, and by society. Begin by living a life that defies expectations. Have the confidence to live life your way. Now, I would love to say that I've always been this confident person, but as I shared with you in my shark story, I've lost it before. We all have. Many of you may have felt insecure or scared when asked to speak up at work. Some of you may have been doing the "fake it till you make it" strategy, but you're finding it exhausting. Most of you just need a slight mindset shift to truly step into your power. And all of you need to realize that confidence is an inside job. It lies within you and you are in complete control of living a very bold life.

I believe there are three types of confidence we need daily:

1. Confidence in our abilities,
2. Confidence in our communication, and
3. Confidence in our outcomes.

Confidence in Our Abilities

I think many people struggle with confidence in their abilities because they're not seeing the proof in what they can do. I think about it like proposal writing. Let's say you are asked to pitch to a client, or maybe you are pitching an idea to your boss, and you know how to write a proposal. You know how to seal this idea. In that moment, you know you have that ability. So if I asked you, "how well can you write proposals?" in this situation you would say, "very well."

The problem is, over time, you have a three-week period where everybody said "no" to your proposal. Your boss hated your last three ideas. And in your head, the negative thoughts begin to appear. You might say to yourself, *Well, I can't write proposals. I have lost my ability to pitch new ideas.*

The truth is you haven't lost it. You've lost <u>confidence</u> in your ability, but you haven't lost the <u>ability</u> to write proposals. One of the things that hold us back is allowing past experiences and other people to determine what we're good at. You are a goal-oriented go-getter, and you are good at many things. And when you focus on your abilities and begin to believe in them, great things can happen.

Strategy #12 Rewrite Beliefs That Aren't Working

Susan is one of my coaching clients. And I wanted to share a little bit about her story because I think it shows how we begin to doubt our abilities. Susan came to me because work wasn't working for her anymore. She wasn't getting promoted. She just knew she should have moved up. And yet, she had been in this job for ten years and was struggling trying to decide, *Do I still need to work here? Should I move on? What's going on?*

Susan didn't like getting passed over for promotion. In our work together, I took her back and we retraced her steps in the Success Model so that we could figure out what was causing her to be passed over. What we discovered when we did that was that Susan's beliefs were the problem.

Over the years, she had gotten passed up for a couple of promotions, which made her start to doubt herself. For years, she had been doubting herself and thinking she wasn't good enough and thinking her boss didn't like her. This vicious cycle activated the emotions of shame, guilt, anger, jealousy, envy, which then initiated her pulling away at work. She stopped engaging with her colleagues. She just did the bare minimum to get by. When Susan didn't go above and beyond anymore, it led to the outcome of...well, let's just say she wasn't in a good position when promotions came around.

When I spoke with Susan, we were able to see that the issue was her beliefs. She had the ability to do the job. She'd had the ability all along. Yes, she could get some extra training, some extra coaching on different skill sets, but she had the ability.

What she didn't have was the belief in herself because she had gotten knocked down too many times. It hurt her too much. She was living in the middle of the hurt.

We took action and we rewrote those beliefs. And by rewriting those beliefs, Susan gained more confidence. She started giving herself more belief in herself and in her abilities. Then new emotions revved up in Susan: excitement, confidence, and feeling in charge. Assertiveness for her confidence equaled courage. That became Susan's feeling word, "courage." So she started to feel courage.

It began when Susan started changing her behaviors. By volunteering for opportunities when they came up, she re-engaged with her coworkers and became more of a team player. Now, I wish I could have just given her the promotion, because darn it, I think she earned it. That hasn't happened...yet. What has happened, though, is Susan's most recent performance review was the best she's had in eight years! And her boss has given her a senior lead position. Even though it's not a promotion, she is now the senior lead on her team. And Susan believes that promotion is in the bag when she gets to that stage.

All of this changed because Susan rewrote a simple belief.

Here's what I want you to think about: Are you really lacking confidence in your abilities and unsure you are capable of something? Or is the issue that you used to have the confidence in the abilities that have slipped away because of something that's happened, because the proof isn't there the way you would want it?

When you decide you're no longer good at something, that belief means you're no longer good at it. For me, as I shared in the introduction, my turning point was in dance. I was good at dancing as long as I was winning. Once I stopped winning, did that magically mean I was a bad dancer? No, but when I stopped winning, I doubted my abilities. Have you heard the expression, "Confidence is an inside job"? I think when we talk about confidence being an inside job, we forget that these beliefs that we have are thoughts that we have carried with us for many years. We've got to rewrite a lot of beliefs. And that takes a lot of effort and this work is very intentional.

Confidence in Our Communication

The second problem area of confidence is communication. Confidence in communication is one of the most common issues we experience. We lack confidence when we're speaking up in front of other people, maybe in front of a group, or we lack confidence when talking in front of a person of authority. Often, we lack confidence when it comes to difficult conversations and when we have to give people feedback. Many of us desire confidence in our communication.

We want to be able to stand up and speak our mind. To our family. To our boss. Possibly even in front of a giant crowd. And that takes confidence. But, more than the confidence to do it...what we are really searching for is confidence that our message will be received. That people will be able to hear us. To truly listen.

Strategy #13 Practice Before You Speak

The main reason why many of us struggle with confidence with our communication is because we're not intentional. When we don't plan what we're going to say and go unprepared into conversations, we are bound to have that moment thirty minutes later where we say to ourselves, "Oh dang! I wish I would have said that!" Most of us have had that moment when the perfect comeback occurs to us— three hours too late!

Confidence in communication comes from planning, knowing what you want to say, and effectively delivering your message. Start by being aware of how you are delivering your messages when you speak. Are you showing up with your shoulders back and your head held high? Are your facial expressions and body language aligned to make sure people understand what you are trying to say? You just have to step up and do it.

For example, if I need to deliver critical feedback to a team member. I want to deliver that with confidence, sharing the issue, identifying a possible solution, and providing positive support. "Hey, this is the direction we're headed, and this is what you need to do differently in the future. And, just so you know, I've got your back." The same applies if I pitch a new proposal or idea to my boss.

Confidence in Our Outcomes

We want and desire confidence in our outcomes. Who wouldn't want a 100% guarantee that what we want to happen will, in fact, happen?

The number one reason we don't have confidence in our outcomes is when we don't have proof that it's ever worked before. It's really easy to have confidence in outcomes when you're doing the same thing over and over and over again getting the same results. If I know that I am driving to my local Target, I can have 100% confidence that my car will get me there. Why? Because I've done it many times. I'm 100% confident in that outcome because I have the prior experience.

What about new experiences? When we don't have proof of what we have done, we start to doubt what we can do. While we can't control what will happen, we can influence outcomes by preparing.

Your past does not dictate your future. Your past is past. You build on your experiences and learn from them. Once you realize everything you've done before is preparing you for making better choices, your confidence can come from another source. Confidence in your outcomes isn't about having done something 10,000 times before. Confidence in your outcomes is about confidence in yourself. It's about knowing that you have done everything in your power to make this happen.

Strategy #14 Prep for Outcome Success

Remember our success model:

Your **B**eliefs activate your Emotions.
Your Emotions influence your **B**ehaviors.
Your **B**ehaviors dictate your Outcomes.
Your **O**utcomes Prove Your Beliefs.

Since beliefs are 25%, emotions are 25%, and behaviors are 25%, that means 75% of the model is 100% in your control. And that last 25%? That last quarter is your outcome. The good news is if you're doing the first 75% right, those outcomes can be guaranteed. The bad news is that most of us lack that knowledge, which threatens our confidence in our outcomes.

If you are aware of and practice using the right behaviors, creating all the right emotions, and having all the right beliefs based on the success model, your outcomes are more guaranteed than they've ever been. That is something you can start building today.

The Cost of Confidence (What is the COST of a Lack of Belief?)

What is the lack of confidence costing you? If you don't have confidence in your abilities, if you don't have the belief in yourself, what are you losing? Are jobs, promotions, or projects slipping through your fingers? Is it costing you money, maybe in your business, and maybe personally in lost salary opportunities? Maybe it's costing you relationships. Maybe you are even practicing self-sabotage. Are you placing the blame on others when all along the lack of confidence was an inside job?

Once you figure out what your lack of confidence is costing you, that's the motivation you need to change those outcomes. You can use this to guide you in doing the hard work, the inner work. This awareness will prepare you to rewrite your beliefs.

Strategy #15 Record Your Proof of Success

Rewriting your beliefs is a simple process, though it may not be easy to do. Step 1 is to examine all of your thoughts. What do you think about yourself, your abilities? Write it all down. Once you feel like you have captured the majority of beliefs, move to the next step.

The next step is to list out the proof. See, for every belief we have about ourselves (good or bad) there is some sort of proof behind it. You have to start listing out your proof. What has happened, what has been said, what outcome makes you feel that these beliefs are true? Now, here's the real work. Proof works both ways, so take a look at the proof for the GOOD beliefs. The beliefs that say you are wonderful, smart, and capable. Write down the proof of those positive beliefs. Feel them. Look at them frequently. I post mine on a sticky note on my bathroom mirror. I recite them aloud every morning. The positive beliefs and the proof that supports them are visible and in front of me daily.

When you rewrite your beliefs and write the proof behind them, they become real in your brain. They shift you into the victorious cycle.

Showing Up Dynamically

In order to make sure that our message is heard, we have to be a dynamic speaker. What does showing up as a dynamic speaker really mean? It means being able to set an intention with your message. To communicate it with confidence and clarity. To believe in yourself. To believe that you need/deserve to be heard. But how do you become a more dynamic speaker?

Strategy #16 Master Your Mantra

My mantra since my swing dancing experience is "be the shark." What does this mantra do for me? This mantra gives me that feeling of belonging, that feeling of confidence, anytime I say it.

I want you to create a mantra for yourself. It can be a phrase. It can be a famous quote. It can just be just one powerful word. Some of the mantras that I know my clients have used in the past are:

Dreams are possible.
There's magic in you.
Pain is weakness leaving the body.

That last quote wasn't a client, by the way. That was the Marine Corps! However, it is a great example of a powerful mantra. "Pain is weakness leaving the body" is motivating when you're in pain. It is helpful to know there are others who have also been in pain.

"But my darling, what if you really could fly?" Words like these inspire. They work like empowering dream magic or pixie dust, right? All of these things could be mantras for you. It's a phrase or a word, something that makes you feel confident, something that you can use to make those feelings just by saying them to yourself. In addition to confidence, saying that mantra conjures that empowerment, that peacefulness, that calm. It is something quick and easy you can use to activate those emotions so you can be on the right track and have the confidence you seek.

First, you start with the mantra to yourself. When I prepare to speak in front of a group, I tell myself, "People need to hear what I have to say." When you start telling yourself that people need to hear what you have to say, you're going to show up and be dynamic. Holy cow, I have got to deliver a message with impact because these people need to hear it! Anytime I'm getting ready for a presentation, saying my mantra is the first thing I do. I remind myself that people need to hear what I have to say. I say it over and over in my head until it's a chant. That repetition triggers my brain to give me some confidence to stand up and speak.

Strategy #17 Picture Your Peeps

The other thing I do before speaking is to imagine my audience.

Who are they?
What are they going through?
How are they struggling today?
How can I be their shining light today?
How can I be the one who helps them get through it?
How can I give them the golden nugget that they share with others?
How can I give them the funny story that they share over dinner
with their family?

I want the people in my audience to have at least one thing that they take away from our time together. To prepare to make this kind of impact on the audience, I want to think about who they are, and what it's going to look like when I am speaking in front of them.

Preparation and visualization are key ingredients to a confident, dynamic performance.

Side note: You may be asking yourself, *"Stevie...what is this all about? I have no interest in being a public speaker. I don't need to stand in front of a crowd. I would just like more confidence when I go to ask my boss for extra time on a project."*

I get it. I really do. I didn't used to think about communication with one person as dynamic speaking, yet it is. The truth is that if you want even just one person to pay attention to you and truly hear your message, you have to keep them interested. We as humans are drawn to distraction, phones, and other thoughts; listening is hard to do. Yet, when the speaker is dynamic. When they engage us. When they show up with intention, we take notice. Even if there is only one other person in the room.

So YES, you want to be a dynamic speaker. And YES, you have to prepare for it. And YES, the act of speaking requires a little extra boost of confidence.

Nervous Energy vs. Enthusiasm

Anytime you're delivering a message, you need to step up with that confidence. What gets in our way is our bodies. Our minds may be willing but our bodies—sometimes they betray us.

Our hands started to sweat or our legs started to bounce. We've all seen people from a distance and can instantly spot their nervous energy. You might see a man pulling on his shirt collar, or maybe you see a woman at the front edge of her seat with a straight back and she is looking straight forward like someone is going to hit her with a two-by-four. We've heard speakers whose voices crack or they get shaky with their words. People will sometimes grip the podium in front of them so tightly that their knuckles turn white.

We can see a lack of confidence a mile away from body language. With confidence and communication, while it starts with beliefs, body language is just as important. Here are two quick ways to make yourself appear more confident when speaking.

Strategy #18 Fix Your Face

First, fix your face. Now, if you were raised by a Southern mama like mine, you've probably heard this phrase before. Or, if you just happen to have a face like mine, and you cannot play poker at all because everything shows, you've probably heard this phrase before. When I was a child, my mother used to say it to me all the time. When we were eating at my grandma's house, I would put a spoonful of food in my mouth, and then did the kid thing of looking funny, my expression telling everyone in the room, *"eww, tastes gross."* She would elbow me in the ribs and say, *"Stevie Dawn, fix your face."*

Here's the big thing: confidence is in our face. And our lack of confidence, well it is also in our face. When you are feeling insecure, do you look down? Do you kind of tug on your lip a little bit? Do you play with your hair? These actions are technically not your face, but they are all around your head. All of these actions make you look like you lack confidence. Even if you've got all the words, and you've got a good message to deliver, nobody's going to listen if your face isn't saying *I'm a confident person.*

Now, I'm not saying always put on a thousand-watt smile, because there are some conversations when that smile is not appropriate. For instance, if you're going to fire someone, do not put on a smile! It does not help. It just looks creepy.

Just think about this: is your face aligned with the message you're trying to convey? The biggest thing is eye contact. If you're able to look somebody in the eye, that demonstrates confidence.

Strategy #19 Bring Your Body Language to Attention

If we want to show confidence, we're going to have to step it up on our body language game, too. Once we fix our faces, the next area to fix is our shoulders. When we have a lack of confidence, we get smaller. Our ears come up to our shoulders. Heck, we start wearing our shoulder blades as earrings! We start making ourselves like turtles and we get really small.

This doesn't portray confidence. We want to take our shoulders and roll them up, back, and down. What this does is gives us a little more space between our chin and our chest. We want to show off our necks.. It tilts our chins a little bit up and we look more confident. In fact, it even helps us to SOUND more confident by lengthening our vocal cords. Crazy, huh?! If you're struggling with communication, realize that our bodies often betray us.

Make sure that you show up ready to go with all of the confidence on your face and in your body, ready to deliver that message. The truth of the matter is that 75% of message interpretation is based entirely on visual cues. People decide whether to listen to you or not based on the visual cues you're giving off. Our body language can help us feel and look more confident in those conversations.

Strategy #20 Pump Up Your Playlist!

The next thing I would do is play a "pump-up" playlist. Yep, I have a "pump-up" playlist of music that gets me pumped up and ready to go! Whether I am going to do a webinar or I am behind the stage before I go out at a conference or go on camera, I play that "pump-up" playlist. It puts that feeling in my body *that I GOT THIS! It's music that makes me want to dance, that gets me energized, that makes me want to jump up and down.* And yes, the song, "Jump Around" by House of Pain is on it. Your "pump-up" playlist must contain all of the songs that make you feel dynamic when you get out there on stage or on camera. The songs have the power to deliver, to get your energy and adrenaline flowing in advance.

The thing that scares all of us when we go to communicate a message is the fact that everybody's staring at us and everybody's judging us. In reality, if you get through all that adrenaline and that hype personally before you ever step foot in that room, it's not going to be a shock. It's not going to scare you, and it's not going to freak you out. You're just going to let the audience pick up on your awesome energy and add to it.

When you're already feeling pumped up in a good way, you turn those potentially anxious feelings into good energy. And your audience will pick up on that energy and feel it too—bonus!

I can hear you asking yourself if this is really necessary before you go to a weekly team meeting or to give an employee feedback...my answer...YES! The truth is that all communication matters. It all works better with confidence and some mojo. No matter how big or small the audience, they deserve your best, so go through the process and WOW them.

The third area where people struggle is with confidence in their outcomes. Now, you've likely heard this phrase before:

What would you do if you knew you could not fail?

Here is the truth. I think most people who are confident know that they're probably <u>going</u> to fail. And yet, despite this, they're just going to keep going.

Why?

People who are confident know that success is built on a pile of failures. I don't think it's about what you would do if you knew you could not fail.

I think it's about what you would do if you would fail and be totally okay with it.

When we talk about not being confident in our outcome, we think to ourselves:

I don't know if it's going to work out.
I don't know if I'm going to get the job.
I don't know if I'm going to get the deal or close the client.

When we're at that point where we're doubting our outcomes, the truth is, we're struggling with control. We're not going to use the F R E A K word (like freaking out) because I don't like that word. I've already told you earlier in this book, and still to this day, I do think winning is everything.

And I think I can control it. I do. I love to control things, but the truth is that confidence and control are not the same thing. Sometimes, we get them confused.

Mistakenly, we think that confidence is knowing the way it's going to turn out. That's wrong. We can only control ourselves. We can't control the outcome. No matter how it turns out, you cannot be confident in what your outcome will be. Confidence comes in knowing that you're going to be okay no matter the outcome. That's the trick to confidence and outcomes.

Remember BEBO? Think back to the Success Model: beliefs to emotions, to behaviors, to outcomes. If you control your beliefs, your emotions, and your behaviors, well, guess what? You are over 75% of the way there to success. Your outcome will be inevitable if you're controlling all the things that you can control.

But so many times we let other people control us, right? We let others tell us what we can and can't do. What we are capable of. No more! The only thing you can control is YOU, so release everything else and focus on owning your ocean. Control yourself, release control over others.

Several years ago, I had the realization that there are three different kinds of people:

1. Ahead of the Moment People

There are people who live ahead of the moment, meaning they are constantly thinking of that next thing on the to-do list or their next meeting. Since they're constantly focused on the future and thinking ahead, they're activating emotions like anxiety, anticipation, fear. Those are the emotions that we activate when we're feeling so rushed.

When we rush, we feel overwhelmed. Did you know that overwhelm has nothing to do with what's happening in the present? Overwhelm tends to be all about what's about to happen in the future that you cannot control. That's why you feel overwhelmed.

For the first twenty years of my life, I was the "ahead of the moment" person, always thinking big. *What's next? What's next? What's next?* Being so focused on the future means there were things that happened to me in my life, in my younger years, that I know occurred, but I don't have any memory of them. Why?

Because I wasn't fully present.

I was too worried about the future, which activated those emotions.

2. Behind the Moment People

The second type of person is the one who is behind the moment. Now, "behind the moment" people are constantly replaying what's already happened. They're always rehashing, going back over conversations, over emails, figuring out what they should have said and what they should have done. Even right now, those of you who are behind the moment might be thinking about something that you should have said ten years ago. The problem is that constantly rehashing is going to activate its own set of emotions, such as regret, shame, guilt, and depression.

Depression lives in the past. Anxiety is living in the future.

For those of you who struggle with depression or with anxiety, you are familiar with these ways of thinking. And I've been both. I've been an "ahead of the moment" person. That's what I was for about the first twenty years. Then I spent another fifteen years being a "behind the moment" person.

Neither one is helpful.

3. In the Moment People

What we want to strive to be is the "in the moment" person. These are the people who are controlling their environments right now because they know that it's within their control. They activate emotions such as surprise, peace, and calm because they're currently in the moment. By living in the present, they're happy whatever happens.

This is our place of joy.

Strategy #21 Discover Your Place of Joy

There are many situations in which we can feel joy if we can be 100% in the moment. Those times when I was fully present in the moment are indelibly written on my brain because they were epic adventures. Often, when we're planning a big trip or preparing for a big event, we get so caught up in the planning and expectations that we forget to just truly enjoy it when it occurs.

My husband and I were on a cruise and had paid lots of money to go swimming with dolphins because it was something I really wanted to do. (By the way, this was before my love affair with sharks happened!) It was pouring down rain, super ugly, and cold, and I'm looking at my husband.

And I am so sad.

I remember thinking, *Oh, my gosh this is going to ruin my dream. I've been dreaming about swimming with dolphins for so long and it's going to be horrible.*

I kept thinking those thoughts, even when the dolphin handlers told us, "Hey, the dolphins don't mind the rain. They're still going to be out here in the water. It's up to you. If you're willing to get out in the water with them, even with the rain, that's great." There was no lightning, no thunder, just rain.

My husband tried to cheer me up. He said, *"It's gonna be good! We still get to go swim with the dolphins."*

I'm like, *"Yeah, but it's dark and it's cold."*

I kept just focusing on everything that was going wrong. Even when we got in the water and we saw the dolphin, I still kept looking at the sky and thinking about how this wasn't what it was supposed to be.

Have you ever felt that way? Being so upset that what you THOUGHT it was going to be (ahead of the moment) didn't add up to RIGHT NOW, and so you are already thinking about how you will be disappointed AFTER?

Just then, I saw another family from our cruise across the water in a different group. These little kids were laughing and screaming with glee and joy over everything that was happening. And I thought to myself, *Why am I not feeling that way? What are they getting out of this experience that I'm not?*

Our group participated in all of the same activities with the dolphin as their group. The dolphin pulls you along on his flipper and he kisses you on the cheek. He even does little somersaults. Really delightful, right? Everybody gets these same fun dolphin activities.

I thought, *Why are these two little kids screaming with glee, so happy, and I'm sitting here just feeling negative?*

That's when I realized I wasn't living in the moment.

I was so concerned with what it wasn't—my perfect vision of a sunny day—that I wasn't looking at what it was.

I thought, *Here I am, in the ocean with the rain. Isn't that a funny story, because, hey, dolphins don't mind the rain! I should be enjoying this moment! Here I am doing something I have wanted to do for years and I'm here with my husband and we're taking all the pictures and oh, my God! What an adventure!*

I took a deep breath, I closed my eyes, and I let go. I let go of all those expectations, of all those thoughts I had about what this experience should be. I allowed myself to be 100% present with what it was. And it was an amazing day. I squealed just like those little kids!

My adventure with the dolphins is the first time I can remember experiencing that feeling. That's the place of joy. It's when everything else goes away. It all drifts away from your mind. You're able to look with clear eyes and a clear heart and feel all of the goodness around you.

And since then, I try to live in the moment every moment I can.

It's about turning off my phone when I go to a restaurant with my husband so that I can have dinner living in the moment with him instead of worrying about who's texting me or what's happening on Instagram.

It's about cage diving with great white sharks. It's going off the grid, having no internet for five days, in order to be 100% present in that moment and make those memories. And it doesn't have to be big things. It's about everything you do being intentional, realizing that the only way you're truly going to feel joy in it is if you give yourself to the experience 100%, allowing yourself to shut off the distractions, thereby shutting off the negative self-talk.

Practice being 100% in that moment and experience it for all that it has to give you. That's where true joy happens. How are you ever going to cultivate joy if you're not paying attention to how you're feeling on the inside? Take out all the rest of the noise and listen to your soul. Listen to your inner child laugh and squeal. Let that bubble up and you will have found your joy.

It's so easy to get stuck in negative ways of thinking. What we need to do, if we truly want to have confidence in our outcomes, is to be fully present.

I want you to think about which type of person you are. Are you ahead of the moment, behind the moment, or in the moment? And by the way, you can be all three depending on the day. It doesn't matter. While I strive to be in the moment, I'm human, and I can easily slip back into being ahead or behind the moment.

I want you to start noticing when your brain starts slipping ahead. Notice when it starts playing reruns. Start bringing it back to the present moment. Some people do it with meditation. Some people do it with therapy. It doesn't matter what you do. It's about doing the healing you need to do and bringing yourself back to the present. Becoming aware of how you experience each moment will make you more confident in your outcomes.

Where would you want more confidence in your life? Would you want more confidence in your abilities, more confidence in your communication, or more confidence in your outcomes?

Strategy #22 Practice Out Loud

The second one is specifically for those of you who feel confidence and communication are your areas in which you need to do the work. I want you to think about how often you practice what you're going to say out loud.

Some people like to make notes. They write stuff down. They visualize it in their minds. But some of us actually practice conversations out loud. As a speaker, I do it every day. Often, I will practice presentations all week long before I present. When I practice, I do it out loud. Why out loud? Because it's muscle memory.

When I say "my muscles," specifically I mean my brain and my throat. When my muscles have memorized what I'm supposed to say, even if my confidence starts to wane, I still have muscle memory to keep me going. When we create muscle memory, even when we feel shaky, our muscles take over. That's what we want to do to have that confidence. So you need to practice.

This works for many situations, not just giving speaking presentations. If you're going to have a difficult conversation with an employee, you need to practice what you're going to say. Practice where you're going to pause, practice giving them a moment when you're going to let them process what you're saying, and practice the questions you're going to ask them. Whether it's in your office with the doors closed, or in your living room where you have space and can walk around, practice it out loud. It is super important to be able to have that confidence. When it's time to deliver that message, you want it to be muscle memory.

Strategy #23 Make Your Highlight Reel

Think back to Strategy #1, Picture Your Ideal Life. Create a highlight reel based off of the list you made. This will be a visual remembrance, like a movie that you can play in your mind.

When you go back to that list you made for Strategy #1, picture each event and accomplishment. Make it a photograph in your mind. Now blend them all together. While making this highlight reel takes time, it is a great way to remind yourself of your greatness any day that your belief starts to wane.

Go ahead and set this book down as I want you to take out a sheet of paper and start on your list immediately, so you can have a highlight reel working for you.

What are your superpowers? Go back through your life, and write down everything. It can be personal or it can be work-related. It can be physical, spiritual, or mental. It doesn't matter what it is. Write down everything on the list and then keep it somewhere you can easily access. Keep it on your phone or on your desk, somewhere. Keep it near your sticky notes.

When we lose confidence in our abilities, it is helpful to have a list that reminds us that we can do hard things, that we've achieved a lot, and that we do have abilities. It helps us feel that confidence and activate those emotions.

Before you have to go and have that nerve-wracking conversation, before you have to get up and present a pitch, before you have to raise your prices and you're scared to hit that button on your website, before you get to all of that, pull out the list, read it, relive it, and re-feel it.

It's super important.

If you're visual, I recommend after you make the list to make it a visual in your head. Think back on each of those memories and put together a little highlight reel. It's kind of like a trailer for a movie that features all of the good parts of your life.

Once you've got your highlight reel, all of the highlights of your life, as many as you can possibly remember, you want to be able to close your eyes and visualize it. Then, you're going to start smiling. You're going to start feeling those emotions, which are going to initiate behaviors that are aligned with confidence and empowerment and peace and exhilaration. It is a wonderful feeling!

Our highlights are always available so we can replay them for ourselves, so we don't forget our inner greatness. For many, forgetting our inner greatness is what holds us back from finding confidence and feeling unstoppable. It's the idea that we've lost faith, that we've lost the ability to do great things. However, each of us can do great things.

Remember at the end of the day, confidence is an inside job and it all starts with you, your beliefs, your emotions, your behaviors, and then your outcomes. I want you to find a way to be the shark in your life starting right now.

Strategy #24 Remember, You Are An Expert

Experts are people who have years of experience, education, certifications, and degrees. They are way far above us with all this expertise! This is what many of us think.

The truth is, to somebody in your world, you are the expert because you know more about a certain subject than they do. You do have to know more than your clients do. Otherwise, you wouldn't be the person delivering the message, having training, or being able to post. In the big view, all of us know more about something than everybody else. We are each an expert in something because it was more important to us in our lives. We spent more time on it. We were interested in it. It was a passionate topic for us. And inevitably, there's somebody else who doesn't have as much expertise as we do.

Let's say you show up at Target every single week. You are there a lot. We might even say you're a raving Target fan, right? After shopping there so frequently, you probably know what is stocked on each aisle. By heart, you know where certain things are in that store. If a stranger walked up to you and asked, *"I'm sorry, do you know where the birthday cards are?"* and you point them towards the cards, in that moment, you are the expert. You know the store and you're able to tell that person, *"Actually, they are at the front of the store, on the right-hand side."* In all things, there's an expert in the room. And so we need to stop putting ourselves down.

When you're struggling to think about yourself as an expert, I want you to remember that. We need to stop saying that we don't have enough education, or we don't have enough training because the truth is you do know something now.

You might argue and say, *"I'm not an expert in what I want."* Maybe you want to be an expert in a topic and you're not there yet. Well, that's great. Knowing that you want to become an expert tells you where you need to focus and put in some effort.

As I shared in the introduction, dance is my life! Here's an insider tip that dance studios would not want you to know: most partner dance studios, like ballroom swing and Latin, that kind of studio, are totally okay hiring you as an instructor as long as you as the teacher knows one move more than what your students are learning this week.

Just one move.

Studios build a whole business model on that one, *know one more move, at least one week ahead of your students.* That's it. Think about that in your life. Is there something in which you are one week ahead of somebody else? Is there an area in which you have that one little bit of additional knowledge more than somebody else? Then you're the expert, and you have the right to call yourself that because you are an expert to somebody else. Now, you may not be the world's greatest expert, right? You may not be the only one in the entire world with your expertise, but you are an expert and it is absolutely okay to position yourself as such.

Whether we think we're an expert or not, it is so important to keep learning. Champions never stop training. The people with the most continue to seek education. The fact that you're taking lessons doesn't mean you're not an expert, however. It just means you're continuing in that journey.

I want to challenge you. When you show up, I want you to show up knowing that you're an expert and that somebody out there, like me, is looking to you and putting you in that place.

So, let's make a deal. You keep showing up, looking that way and I'll keep thinking, *You're that expert.*

Make sure you look at someone who shows up consistently if you want to learn how to keep doing it. Look at how other people in your industry are positioning themselves. What makes you think they're an expert?

If you are feeling down on yourself for not being an expert in everything, I want you to think: how would it feel to actually be the person who knows everything, the person who has no more to learn, and who has no other mentors? If you had no other person to learn from, I think that would be really scary and terrifying. Most of us want to know that we can continue to grow and learn. I encourage you to continue to seek out mentors, who are your experts, to learn from. And always remember that you are the expert for somebody coming up behind you.

I feel the words of the song, "Greatest Love of All" by Whitney Houston, really capture the essence of what it means to be an expert.

> *"...The greatest love of all*
> *Is easy to achieve*
> *Learning to love yourself*
> *It is the greatest love of all."*

Checklist for Bold Confidence

- Evaluate your confidence in your abilities, communication, and outcomes
- Rewrite beliefs that aren't working
- Practice before you speak
- Prep for outcome success
- Record your proof of success
- Identify and master Your mantra
- Picture your peeps
- Fix your face
- Bring your body language to attention
- Pump up your playlist
- Discover your place of joy
- Practice out loud
- Make your highlight reel
- Remember that you are an expert

CHAPTER 5
EMOTIONAL RESILIENCE AND SUCCESS

MANY YEARS AGO, I saw a speaker do something quite incredible. In front of a group of about 200 people, he walked to the front of the stage and held up a $20 bill. And he said, *"Raise your hand if you want this $20 bill!"* And 200 people raised their hands. No surprise there, right? Then, the speaker took the $20 bill and crumpled it up in his hands. And he said, *"How many of you still want the $20 bill?"* Everybody's hand was still in the air. Next, he took the $20 bill, threw it on the floor, and ground into it with his shoe heel. At this point, the $20 bill was looking a little torn and grubby. And he's like, *"Last chance, who wants it?"*

Every last hand in the audience of 200 went up in the air.

Then he said something that I will never forget.

"You just learned a very important life lesson. No matter what I did to the $20 bill, it still has value. It is still worth $20. You still want it because it still has value to you. No matter what it looked like, even when it was crumpled up.

We are like that $20 bill. There are going to be things that happen that you don't want to happen. There are going to be decisions you have to make *and consequences. And there's going to come a time where you feel worthless, crumpled up. When life has dug its heel into you. The truth is, no matter what happened to you before, no matter what will happen to you in the future, you still have value. You are still worthy."*

Life sometimes makes us feel like a crumpled up $20 bill. I tell that story in every presentation and coaching session I deliver on emotional resilience.

Strategy #25 Practice Resilience

Resilience is about getting knocked down and getting back up again.

These emotionally deflating times happen to all of us. Some of us bounce back easily and get back on board with our dreams. A few of us may have pushed the pause button and sat back, waiting for a sign that everything was going to be okay before we continued. But what all of us know is, *"It's not about how many times you get knocked down. It's about how many times you get up again."* Now, that's not an original quote. That's a quote from Vince Lombardi. Just so you know, dear reader, I am a football girl. So I am allowed to quote him.

Let's take a quick pulse check.

As you are reading this book, how are you feeling today on a scale between 1 and 10, where 1 is crapola and 10 is on top of the world? Go ahead. Say it out loud.

I want you to know that wherever you are right now, however you are feeling, it is okay. It is okay to have a 10 day and equally okay to have a 2 day. And we ALL have had a 2 day before. The truth is that our number can change in an instant. One phone call from your mother-in-law, one email from your boss, can do it. One moment where you spill coffee on your white pants. And that high 8 you were feeling drops way down into a 3.

The trick is, how do we get it back to that high 8? How do we bounce back from those moments?

While you likely already know that emotional resilience is important, there's some background we need to discuss.

Over a third of all employees say that work is a significant source of stress in their lives.[1] Businesses spend $190 billion a year trying to combat stress-related issues.[2] And stress is one of the number one reasons why we talk about emotional resilience. Emotional resilience allows us to handle stress more effectively and more efficiently so that we can get back to a productive way of being, whether it's us being productive in work or productive in our lives.

Emotional resilience and success are intertwined because all of us know that success doesn't happen by ourselves. And we also know that success isn't easy. There are going to be times you get knocked down. There are going to be times that people don't support you. There are going to be times when you need the support. There's going to be a lot of failure on that road to success. And that's why we have to learn to bounce back, keep going, and achieve unstoppable success. I'm sharing this quote from the character Rocky Balboa because it epitomizes the concept of resilience.

> *"Let me tell you something you already know. The world ain't all sunshine and rainbows. It's a very mean and nasty place, and I don't care how tough you are, it will beat you to your knees and keep you there permanently if you let it. You, me, or nobody is gonna hit as hard as life. But it ain't about how hard ya hit. It's about how hard you can get hit and keep moving forward. How much you can take and keep moving forward. That's how winning is done!"*
> — Sylvester Stallone, <u>Rocky Balboa</u>

If you've seen the movie *Rocky* then you know he is the poster boy for hitting back hard in life! When I was researching emotional intelligence during my doctoral degree, I came across a list of eight traits for emotional resilience, and over the years, they have become my bedrock. The eight things I can lean on when times get tough. To be honest, getting my doctoral degree in and of itself was a lesson in resilience. I wanted to quit more times than I could count, but it was the traits of support, humor, and perseverance that kept me going. As I list out the eight traits below, I want you to consider which of these you already possess.

Emotional Resilience: 8 Traits That Make You Feel Great

1. Emotional Reframing

Earlier, I described how we often judge our bodies critically. When you stand in front of the mirror, do you think negative thoughts, such as *I am too fat, I need to lose weight,* or *I look awful?* When I began thinking this way, I knew I had to stop the feelings. I actually did a physical motion which was to hold out my hand as if I were stopping a car in traffic. I said to myself, *Hold on, wait a second. Let's reframe those thoughts. I'm strong. I'm a dancer. Look at what I've overcome.*

As I said that in the mirror, I stood taller. I looked stronger. I began getting confident. I even felt like I could conquer something, which led to me working out! And trust me, this isn't easy. I know a lot of people get those happy endorphins from working out. That's not me. I have to feel good in order to work out. I have to trick myself into it!

I did work out which led to the results I wanted. The next day, when I'm looking in the mirror now, I have reframed my thoughts into saying, *Hey, yeah, I am strong. I can do this now.* I'm reaffirming my positive cycle. Remember The Success Model can be vicious or victorious, it is up to you to choose.

Emotional reframing allows us the ability to truly change our emotions, our actions, and our results. When we're able to reframe those negative thoughts into positive ones, we're able to bounce back. I want you to know this reframing doesn't happen quickly, as this takes effort and practice. You may be in a negative cycle for an hour or a day or a week. The trick is to get out of it as quickly as possible by realizing you're in it.

Number one, stop the feelings. Once you feel those negative feelings creeping over you, I want you to stop feeling and start thinking. Analyze your thoughts, like we did with the mirror example, reframe as needed, and then feel all the feelings that come with the positivity. Change your mindset, change your life.

2. Emotional Awareness

Emotional awareness is the ability to identify when we're feeling these emotions and to be able to categorize them. Do you know the difference between anger and frustration? Do you know the difference between happiness and joy? People who have a high level of emotional awareness can tell exactly what they're feeling. And not only that, but they usually are also people who can tell exactly what somebody else is feeling. This ability makes them amazingly empathetic, which is a great trait for communication, leadership, and success. That's an amazing trait to develop. If you are already good at reframing, if that's already a skill you have, you probably also have emotional awareness because they kind of go hand in hand.

In order to increase your emotional awareness, consider writing down the different feelings you have every day in a small notebook or journal. Identify the feeling. Write down what triggered that feeling to occur. I have worked with my clients who came to me saying, "I am dead inside. I just don't have feelings." That isn't true. We all have feelings. It is just about becoming more in tune with them. Your feelings may not display the same way as others, but that doesn't mean they aren't there.

3. Perseverance

I love sharks. When I think of perseverance, I think of the phrase "just keep swimming" (from *Finding Nemo*, anyone?). "Just keep swimming," is literally a life imperative for sharks. When sharks stop swimming, they stop breathing. Moving forward is how they get oxygen over their gills. If they're not swimming, they're dying.

Wow! Let's take a moment and think about that. What if you had to move to get oxygen? Like right now, you may be sitting down reading this book, not moving at all, yet you are still breathing. That doesn't work for great white sharks. They have to be moving. I often consider, how would my life be different if the only way I could get oxygen was if I had to be moving?! Wow, right?! I would be so thin! In terms of emotional resilience, I think of the $20 and how it still has value no matter its shape. I think of continuing to push forward to get oxygen...to my body, to my soul, to my spirit. You know I like mantras, so "just keep swimming" works for me, but whatever you need to do to cultivate your don't-give-up-ness, do it.

4. Internal Control

Internal control is kind of a fancy way of saying people who try really hard not to be the victim. They look at their lives as if they have control over it. In their viewpoints, life happens for them, not to them. People who have that idea of personal control over their lives, especially in combination with the Success Model, are able to truly see that since they have control, they can bounce back faster. When something negative happens to one of these people, or a situation occurs, they can bounce back because they know they're in control of their lives.

If I can be 100% honest with you, this one is hard for me. I can play the blame game really well. It was her fault for not getting that done on time. It was their fault for not choosing my product. "Those things" are the reason I didn't get what I wanted. Truly, I can be a master of it. But, if we want to be more resilient and to feel better about all of our situations, we have to be willing to give up the blame and focus on an internal locus of control. We have to own it. Own our decisions. Own our consequences. Own our lives.

Here's another mantra for you that I use to feel this trait more frequently in my life: own your ocean.

5. Optimism

If you're able to see the silver lining, if you're able to see the good in situations, it's easier for you to feel emotional stability and to get up to that level of feeling like an 8 again, right? If we felt like the 8 and then we dropped down to a 2, people with optimism are able to bounce back to that 8 a little bit faster.

Optimism can be hard to cultivate because our brains are wired to show us the negative. Our brains are there to remind us of the bad so that we protect ourselves, so that we stay safe. However, we know that risk is a necessary part of success. And we know that living in the past, rehashing old mistakes, is not going to take us into a bright future. If you want to be more optimistic, you have to focus on reframing. Take those negative reminders from your brain, say "thank you for showing me this," and then try to replay a fond memory. Something fun. Something that might show you what could be possible. When we can see more of the sunny part of life, we can be more optimistic that sunny days are ahead.

6. Support

We all know that people who are successful didn't get there by themselves. They had to fail and pick themselves back up over and over again. And a lot of that happened because they had support.

Do you have a circle? Do you have a group of co-workers, friends, family, and other people who support your success and your well-being? When you have that support, it's easier to bounce back. Research shows us that people who have support also provide that kind of support for others.[3] See, support is a two-way street. If you are able to give that support to others, you will be able to receive that support as well. Those of you that are in leadership positions, are business owners, who lead at church or in other hobbies that you do, when you are feeling that support in yourself, you're more likely to give that support to somebody else.

Take time to listen to others. Be a cheerleader. Remind them of their greatness. When you spend the time and effort on them, they are likely to do the same. We all need support. We need people to support us when we fall down. To remind us of our greatness. So, give in order to receive.

7. Humor

People who are able to find the fun to laugh at themselves and at the situation tend to bounce back faster. I don't think there is a lot of explanation needed with this trait. When you laugh, you feel better. When you are able to laugh even during the tough times, you will bounce that number back quicker. Humor is imperative to resilience.

8. Spirituality

When we look at successful people, many claim to have some sort of belief in a higher power, some kind of faith, some kind of thing that is bigger than themselves that they believe in which helps them with their success. And that belief helps them to bounce back when things are tough.

While I am not a super religious person, I do know this trait to be true. In the darkest of times, when life seems to be pushing me into the dirt, it is my faith that gives me light. That gives me a direction.

Let's review…

The 8 traits of emotional resilience are:

1. Emotional reframing
2. Emotional awareness
3. Perseverance
4. Internal Control
5. Optimism
6. Support
7. Humor
8. Spirituality

YOU ALREADY HAVE some of these 8 traits in your toolbox. That is the best part of emotional resilience…you already possess at least two or three of these traits. You can call upon them when you need it. When you are having a bad day. In a bad mood. Or getting anxious about an upcoming stressful event.

Which of these do you have? Which of these traits can you use? Which do you want to develop? When we know what we already have, we can use it to obtain even more success and even more resilience. And when we know more that we want to develop, we can try them out and practice them.

Anytime you're feeling down, anytime you feel like life has crumpled you up like that $20 bill, I want you to lean into the things you already have working for you. So for me, I often use reframing, perseverance, and support. So when I'm feeling down, I can say to myself, *"Stevie Dawn, you are the shark. Just keep swimming."* (*persever-ance*). I have that quote printed everywhere. It's on a sticky note on my desk. I have a t-shirt that says it, and I even have a poster on my wall to remind me.

When I'm having a hard day, I use my support. I call my friends and my family and I say, *"Hey, I just need somebody to tell me it's all going to be okay."* They do that for me. Whatever support you have already, that's what you want to lean into in those tough times.

AND, I use The Success Model a lot. It helps me to reframe my thoughts and change my outcomes.

When you get into those moments when it's getting difficult, when life is getting hard, when everything is really weighing on you, you have to learn how to look at your thoughts.

Strategy #26 Identify Reality from Perception

What happens to many of us is that we live under perceptions. When I feel overwhelmed and think, *Oh, my gosh, everything is piling up on me,* that's a perception. What's the reality? I always get it all done. It's always fine. It's not going to kill me. That's the reality. So, I've got to challenge those thoughts. Here's something you can do today to start.

Take out a blank sheet of paper. Write all the things you think about yourself, and fill up a page with all kinds of thoughts.

After you have written them down, I want you to look at those and ask yourself which are real and which are perceptions. The secret is once you start focusing on what's real, you realize that you are completely capable, that you can absolutely do this. That you've always done the things you've done before. You're going to find that you could start reframing really easily because the distinction between perception and reality is part of the reframing technique. Begin by asking yourself: *what is real? What does the past tell me about myself?*

The past just tells us what's happened. We need to learn from our past, but we do not have to allow the past to dictate our future. Our past has very little to do with our future. So, with that in mind, ask yourself again: *what does the past tell me about myself?*

Continue with your questions. *What do I want to believe about myself?* Start asking yourself positive questions. Don't ask yourself about all the things that can go wrong. Ask yourself about all the things that can go right, right? That's where your power really lies.

Challenge your thoughts and start getting comfortable with challenging yourself. I have to let you know that challenging your thoughts can feel really weird in the beginning if you've never tried this before! With practice it will feel more natural to you. Challenging your thoughts will give you the ability to reframe on the fly when you need to. Using the Success Model, you take action and you do it. You reframe more quickly because you already know the truth versus what you've been telling yourself in the negative cycle.

Next, validate and refocus. This is kind of a "twofer," right? We're going to talk about it in two different ways. We're going to talk about validating and refocusing yourself. And I'm also going to teach you a skill for validating and refocusing with other people. Many of you not only need to be emotionally resilient, but you really want to help other people around you to be emotionally resilient. It's frustrating when you see people around you struggling in this negative cycle. You want to help them to get out of it! Validate and refocus are exactly how you help them.

First, let's talk about you. Validate and refocus means accepting that the feelings you're feeling are okay and not adding to the negativity.

Let's say that I'm feeling sad because I lost a client. That sucks, right? And as a result of losing that client, I am feeling sad about it.

Strategy #27 It. Is. Totally. Okay. To. Feel. Sad

What's not okay is to feel guilty about feeling sad! One emotion at a time is plenty. But how many of us have done that? You felt over-whelmed and then you felt guilty for feeling that way. Or you felt worse because you think, Oh, my God, now I'm taking out how I am feeling on other people.

Start by validating that that emotion is there. If you learn nothing else, please make the commitment to yourself that you're going to only allow yourself one negative emotion at a time. And you're going to try not to add on. Layering negative emotions just pushes us into the negative cycle. We don't need to be there.

You've got to validate. Recognize that it's okay to feel sad. Some-times, I give myself a time limit. I can have a five-minute pity party. Pity, pity, pity. I wallow for five minutes and that's it!

Now, it's time to refocus, but we have to validate that our feelings are okay because how many of us at some point in our life have been told, *Oh, just stop feeling like that. Just stop feeling that way.* Well, gosh, if just stopping the feelings were that easy, we'd all be doing it.

We can't just stop first. We have to accept it first. *Okay. I'm feeling this way. Got it. I'm feeling it. Now. Let me reframe.* After you validate your feelings, it is time to refocus on something else.

Imagine this: I'm working with a gentleman named Bob and I have a meeting to go over plans for our next event. And in this meeting, Bob starts off by saying, *"I think we need to use blue placemats,"* and I say, *"I think we need red."* In those two statements, unless someone gives in, we are now at an impasse. Where we're headed is into having an argument, right? We're going to have some kind of conflict about this red-blue thing.

How do I stop this negative vibes train wreck? What I have to do is implement a communication strategy. I have to validate Bob that his feelings are good, and let him know that his thought process is fine. And then I need to refocus. So imagine how it feels when instead Bob says, *"I think we need to use blue placemats,"* and I say, *"You know what, Bob, I get that. I can see how blue placemats would work. But I wonder if we've thought about how red would work. I wonder if there's another color that could be better for our brand."*

Do you see what I did there? I validated Bob before I gave my own opinion. What happens to a lot of us is that we see somebody in a negative cycle. We know they need to bounce back. What we end up doing is just trying to help them refocus without the validation. The way the other person hears this is, *"Okay. Just get over it."* No one likes to hear that.

That phrase makes me think back to my Marine Corps days. I had a drill sergeant who used to say, *"Suck it up, buttercup,"* for what felt like every five seconds in the beginning. 'Cause you know, boot camp is hard. I would never say this to a drill sergeant, but I used to think, *"Hey, does that really work for anybody? Suck it up buttercup."* I didn't find it motivating. She would've been better to say, *"I get that. It's hard. I see that you're struggling (validation). Let's focus on moving to the next level. Let's focus on that next three mile hike we've got to do."* If she had validated and then reframed it, I might've bought in a little bit more.

We have to think about this reaction when somebody is in this negative cycle and we want to help them out of it. Remember that just saying, *"Get over it. Just let it go. It's no big deal,"* isn't effective. What we have to be willing to do is to validate that what they're feeling is okay, and then refocus them onto something else. That's one of the key things you can do for yourself and for everyone else around you.

Strategy #28 Embrace Self-Compassion

Self-compassion is the idea that you actually treat yourself as somebody who's worthy of love and caring and support. Often, we are our own worst critic, meaning we treat ourselves worse than we would treat anybody else. Self-compassion starts with creating a judgment-free zone for yourself, allowing yourself no judgment as you go through life. And that's okay, except that you're going to make mistakes. Things inevitably aren't going to go well, but you're going to get back up again, right? It's okay to fall down. It just matters that you get up.

The second part of self-compassion is having grace and acceptance. And that means being accepting of where you are and knowing that you are on the path to where you want to be.

I think about grace and acceptance a lot, especially when I think about this idea of success and achieving goals and accomplishment, which we all want. There's lots of things you have to do to achieve those goals in those accomplishments. But somehow, we only reward ourselves for achieving the big goal. We don't reward ourselves for all the things along the way. If we go back to my example about working out, if I only ever felt better when I actually had lost the 15 pounds, I would never lose the 15 pounds. To get myself to the goal, I had to celebrate every little step. I've got to celebrate every workout, y'all! Every time I get on my Peloton bike my husband gives me a fist bump and that's like, *"Yeah, we got on the bike!"* If we wait till we hit the end goal to celebrate, we will never hit the end goal. And let's face it. When you do hit the goal and you celebrate the celebration, it lasts for like five seconds and then you move on with life. We have to learn to celebrate along the way, and that's grace and acceptance.

Strategy #29 Write Your Own Permission Slip

We must stop waiting for permission from other people. We have to learn how to write our own permission slip. Too often, we just sit and wait. Wait for something to happen to us. Wait for someone to tell us it is okay to go forward, to change direction, to make a decisions. But, YOU are the only one who has to live YOUR life. Just you. So you get to be in charge. You get to make the choices. You are in charge. Therefore, the only permission who needs to sign your permission slip is you.

You don't need to ask for somebody's permission to want more from your life. You don't need to ask for somebody's permission to want to achieve that promotion, to go after that new job, to start a side hustle, whatever you want!

Sometimes, bouncing back from a difficult situation is really all about telling ourselves it's okay to bounce back. It's okay to move on. When we deal with grief, it's okay to move on. It's okay to move forward after we have addressed it, and it's okay to close that chapter.

Checklist for Emotional Resilience and Success

- Remember the eight traits for emotional resilience:

1. Emotional Reframing
2. Emotional Awareness
3. Perseverance
4. Internal Control
5. Optimism
6. Support
7. Humor
8. Spirituality

- Practice resilience
- Identify reality from perception
- Remember: It. Is. Totally. Okay. To. Feel. Sad.
- Embrace self-compassion
- Write your own permission slip

CHAPTER 6

CAPTIVATING VISIONS—MORE SPECIFIC VISION

Defining Your Success

OUR PERSONAL DEFINITIONS of success are important because we can't let anybody else define our business. I think that sometimes as entrepreneurs, we get trapped in definitions of success by other people. Other people's definition of success may be earning $10K per month. Other people's definition may be earning a half-million dollars a month. Other people's definition of success may be just paying this month's bills.

While everybody has a different definition of success, we get wrapped up in some of the promotion and marketing materials out there. We start comparing ourselves to others in our space, wondering if we're not as successful because we haven't reached the levels that they're talking about.

Strategy #30 Define Success For Yourself

When I started my business, my definition of success was just, Can I replace the corporate income I used to make? I wrote down the numbers. Here's the number of dollars I was making as a corporate employee. Here's what I would like to make right now as an entrepreneur. That was my definition of success. I felt once I reached that, that was good. That was golden. I was okay at that level, at that number.

What I found though over the years over time is my definition of success kept changing. I didn't hit that goal until year three, but I hit that goal. And then, I hit a goal hole. I thought, Okay, well what's next? Do I consider myself successful now? Or am I still trying to achieve something? Then, I would set another goal.

"Hey, I need to cross the six-figure mark. Hey, I need to cross the quarter of a million mark. Now we're focused on half a million." Every time I reached a goal, I set another one. The trick is, my definition of success may have changed over the years, but that baseline level of success should still make me feel successful.

Think about this: if you set this goal, and then you reach it, then aim for the next goal, have you now forgotten that you were already successful once? Success is a tricky thing. We keep chasing it, pretending like what we've already done doesn't count, and that's not true. I have been successful since year three because that's when I hit that baseline definition of success.

I've been successful ever since then. I mean, in essence, most of us have probably been successful since way early in our lives, but somehow we stop saying it, we stop thinking about it. We start thinking, Until I reach that next goal, I am now not successful. No, you're still successful at reaching the previous goal. You just have a new one to strive for. That's okay. You're still successful.

I want you to identify your personal definition of success. How do you know that you achieved it? How do you keep growing without losing that inner monologue that says, I am still successful? We never want to lose that just because we're chasing new and bigger and better goals.

Success is achieving your own goals. It is not about what everyone else thinks. It is not worrying about what somebody else's goals will be. You have to define it for yourself. It does me no good as a coach to support somebody in growing their business if I'm just pushing them to grow it to what I think it should be. It's not my definition of success that matters. It's theirs.

Strategy #31 Track Each Step of Your Journey

Tracking where you were is important so you can see how far you have come. I think it's really important that we write down our goals so we can refer back to that document. How often do you go back, look at where you were five years ago, see your growth, and remind yourself how successful you are? Usually, we just look at the last year, when we have to do taxes, right?

When you look at five years of growth, that probably looks pretty incredible. Are you going back and recognizing your success? Are you able to look back and see how far you've grown and celebrate? Understanding what success means to you and what success means to your business is essential for your business's success. You've already achieved a ton till now to get to where you are.

Instead of just looking at how far you have left to go, let's make sure you are still taking time to look backward and say, "But look how far we've come!"

If we don't know where we're going, how will we ever know if we get there? If we truly want unstoppable success, we have to know what that looks like. Often, we become stuck in the rut of where we currently are and what's currently happening instead of really looking at where we're going. You might say, *"I am great at setting goals."* Goals are good, but vision is better, because a goal can be changed or tweaked if you don't meet it. A vision is absolute. A vision tells you what to do and not do in your life. A vision can be used to help you make decisions. A vision gives you the overall picture of what your unstoppable success is going to lead you. A vision is what motivates you to get out of bed every day and show up for you for your dreams and your goals.

I spent years of my life chasing after goals. They were good goals. I achieved them. I even wanted to achieve them, and yet, I didn't love what my life looked like when I got there. The truth was that I had no vision. I didn't really have a long-term plan. I didn't know where I was headed. I just kept adding more rungs to the ladder and kept climbing.

It wasn't until I had multiple failed relationships, a career that had become boring, and no spirit left that I started to think, *Maybe something is missing.* When I was staring in the mirror wondering where that other girl, that old me, had gone...that was when I realized that I had no vision. I had stopped dreaming.

I think we do that a lot. As children, we are all about the dreams, the impossible. Yet, into adulthood we get told to check the boxes. Get the career, the house, the husband, the family...check the boxes and you will be successful. Which led me to feel depressed. Which led me to ask the question...whose definition of success?

See, I was defining success based on society's definition, not my own. I had no idea what success looked like, and so I had to take a deep and dark look at myself. The real Me. The one hiding underneath all those expectations. Stevie. What did she think success was? How did she define it? What did it look like? It was in answering these questions that my life started to change. It started to have more direction. More color. More life. It became MY life. Not theirs. I became...myself...again.

How do you define success?

The easiest way to create your own definition of success is to be able to VISUALIZE it. To capture a vision of your future that makes you want to get up every day and chase after it.

Let's focus on how to create a captivating vision for yourself. The first step that you have to do is knowing what that vision looks like. After you read the list of questions below, set this book and everything else down. Get your hands free. Relax. I want you to close your eyes and paint a picture of your future. Imagine your whole Life, put yourself in the middle of that picture, turn 360 degrees around. See everything that is there.

- What does your work look like?
- Who is in your picture with you?
- What hobbies are you partaking in?
- What activities are there?
- How are you connected with your spirit?
- How is your health and your vibrancy, your vitality?
- Hey, what clothes are you wearing? Are you comfy? Are you dressed up in a ball gown?
- Where are you? Is it sunny? Is it cloudy? Are you in the mountains? Are you on a beach?
- If you look around 360 degrees, what are you doing?
- What is happening in your life? What do you see?
- How do you feel now?

Open your eyes, take out a sheet of paper and jot down anything that came to you. Absolutely anything, there is no judgment. There are no bad answers here. Write down absolutely everything that came into your mind.

We want to make that picture get as crystal clear as humanly possible. And we're going to achieve that through four steps.

Strategy #32 Ask Yourself a Bazillion Questions

You're going to ask yourself a bazillion questions here that you've never even thought of asking. You're going to ask yourself where you want to be in your future.

What's the weather like?

What are you looking at?

What are you wearing?

These may seem like really "out there" questions, but let's be honest with ourselves. If your vision of your perfect life, you dream you're staring at mountaintops, well, that's probably not happening in the middle of Kansas. Nothing against Kansas. I lived there for a while. I went to Wichita State University—go Shocks! But if mountains are in your vision, then this may not be the right place for you.

That doesn't mean you move tomorrow, but it does mean you have to start making decisions to get you to that place you want to be. Maybe your vision wasn't one place. Maybe it was multiple places because you look at part of your vision as being able to travel. That's great. Then you're going to have to make decisions that get you there.

How about your clothes? Do you want to be in a place where you have to wear a power suit every day? Or do you want to be in a place where you can wear yoga pants as your work uniform? Let's face it, if you HATE doing your hair and makeup every day, maybe in your vision you work someplace where your uniform can be all black athletic gear. Cool! How can you make that happen?

It's important to know this is about your vision. It's not about what society told you. This is about you and what you authentically want, not what others have told you that you want. Part of this research involves asking questions about who's around you. Who in your family do you still see in your vision? Who do you "paint" into the picture with you? Who do you not include and why? Sometimes, we do not think people are going to be there in our future in order for us to feel like our life may be closer to our vision. We need to break off toxic relationships and open a space for great relationships. Maybe you, in your vision, have a person standing next to you holding your hand, but you can't see their face yet because you haven't met them yet. That's okay, as it's important to know what you want.

For me, when I was crafting my vision, I realized there were never any children. I don't want kids. That's not for me. But society told me I was supposed to. And I had that goal for so long that once I realized, when I started "painting" my vision picture, that kids weren't in it and that was okay. I started making changes to my goals based on my vision.

Who is with you? How are you contributing to your vision? Many of us think about our future and sometimes we imagine retirement. I don't want you to go that far because that's going to be a different vision and you're going to get there soon enough. I want you to paint this vision of the next five to ten years. And if that is retirement for you, that's totally okay. But for some readers, you're still working.

How are you contributing? How are you working? What are you doing? Are you sitting in an office building or are you sitting at a coffee shop? Are you sitting on a park bench? How are you contributing to the community? How are you impacting the world? I believe all of us have a purpose, something we are uniquely designed to do by God's grace. I want you to think about what is around you. How are you contributing? How are you being impactful? What hobbies and activities do you do? Do you see yourself in a pair of skates? Do you see a basketball in your vision? Do you consider those things important to you?

Once you've done this research, take a deep breath. Then, I want you to feel that vision. How does it make you feel? Does it make you feel good? Does it make you feel excited, motivated, inspired, peaceful, calm, relaxed, happy? One of the biggest pitfalls that people have when they're answering these questions and doing this research, is they judge their own answers. You cannot let negative thoughts creep in. It's your dream! And nothing can be wrong in a dream.

Nothing is too much, too wonderful, too big. Anything you want is possible.

> *"Is it possible*
> *That the square root of impossible is me?"*
> *—Square Root of Possible by Madelin Mills*

Strategy #33 "Paint Your Own Picture"

Once you've done the research and you've started really writing it out, now you can start painting that picture. Have you ever made a vision board? I'm a big believer in vision boards. Candidly, I just don't love the whole having to find magazines that have the right pictures and cutting them out and gluing them on. It is a little too crafty for my taste. But with new technology, I make my vision boards using photos online and then make it the wallpaper for my desktop. I literally stare at my vision board all day long, every day.. You must be able to picture your vision.

My vision board….well, In my photo vision board, I have a picture of my husband and me in 2017. We are sitting, laughing, and smiling. That's in my vision, that happiness, that joy, my marriage. I also have a photo of a cruise ship. I love to cruise, and I want to go on at least one cruise a year. I also have a photo of a wonderful group of women that was taken at a winery. We did a wine tasting and just had a night of fun. It's really important to me in my vision that I'm surrounded by my friends. Seeing family is important to me, too. And my family is there, but at the end of the day, it's my friends that are featured predominantly in my vision, and that's reminding me to make sure I make time for them. And that we are standing arm in arm, hugging each other, no matter what.

One of the things that's in my vision is a stage spotlight. I want to be on a stage impacting millions. When I asked myself, *"What is my impact? How am I contributing to my community?"* my answer was that I wanted to convince a million people that they could have every dream they've ever wanted. That's my impact. That's what I want to do. My vision of a stage spotlight signifies that for me that energy and inspiration.

So that's a little bit of my vision. What's yours?

After you've done all the research and included what is important to you in your vision, I want you to start finding pictures. You can do the poster board and the magazines vision board, or use a photo vision board. The how doesn't matter. What's important is that you take the time to write the words, envision the pictures, and include your big goals and big dreams. There is no wrong way to do this. What counts is that you need to paint the picture for yourself and not for anyone else. You need to have your vision in front of you every day, some way, some shape, somehow. Whether it's on your phone, on your computer, on a piece of paper, on a poster board, wherever, you need to be able to see it every day to remind yourself why you're working so hard and why you're moving forward. So the second step is to find that picture.

Strategy #34 Know Your Habits

Habits are what we repeatedly do. It's what we repeatedly think, what we repeatedly feel, what we repeatedly take action on, and what we repeatedly get. Those are all habits.

We have thinking habits. We have feeling habits. We have actions that we take that are habits. What you need to make sure of is that your habits are leading you to that vision.

If you look at your vision and you say, "*Okay, I see a soccer ball and a soccer goal. I want to play more soccer. I want to join a co-ed team,*" next, ask yourself if you are doing things every week that are going to get you there. Are you working out? Are you finding a co-ed team? Are you practicing? What are you doing? You will only make that vision a reality if you adopt habits. If you work every day to get to that goal.

Often, we have so many bad habits that we're not actually getting where we want to be. We have to be relentless and look at everything we're doing and everything we're not doing. And we have to make choices. Our habits will help us achieve that vision, but only if we pay attention to them.

Ask yourself what small steps you can take. Here are a list of questions to kickstart your thinking:

- What mantras do you need to start?
- What do you need to tell yourself?
- Do you need to be telling yourself, *"I can do it"*?
- Do you need to be telling yourself, *"I'm beautiful?"*
- Do you need to be telling yourself, *"I'm confident?"*
- What do you need to be saying to yourself?
- How can you map out how you're going to get to this vision, and how it's going to end up working for you?
- How will you implement the changes you need to make?
- What's not going well for you?
- What's holding you back?
- What's getting in the way?
- What do you need to stop doing because it's taking you away from that path?
- What do you need to start doing to make those visions a reality?
- What goals do you need to set?
- How are you going to stay motivated?
- How are you going to measure your success?
- How do you know when the vision comes true? Or when pieces of the vision come true?
- What's your measurement for determining when your vision comes true?
- What are your obstacles? What's going to get in your way? What's going to hold you back from achieving this vision that you want?

- What expectations do you need to be setting for yourself, for your family at work in your business so that you make sure that vision can come true?

Too often, we end up doing things because somebody else told us those were the things we were supposed to do to make ourselves happy. Somebody else told us that was the direction we needed to take. But if that direction you're going, that goal you're trying to achieve, doesn't line up with your overall vision, stop and ask yourself, *"Why am I doing this?"* And stop!

Don't get me wrong. Sometimes your boss may tell you, *"You've got to do something. You just gotta do it."* I get it. That one might be out of your hands. But there's so much of our life that is up to us, that we have control over if we would just look at what we really want and what we need to do.

The biggest pitfall I see with my clients at this step is that they start worrying about what other people think. Does your husband understand your vision? If your kids understand your vision, does your boss understand your vision? Do your friends understand your vision?

Guess what?

It doesn't matter.

I don't say that to be harsh. I just want you to be real in this moment. This is your life. Nobody else gets to live it. This is your vision. Nobody else needs to see it. All that matters is that you know where you're headed and what's going to matter to you. You'll have a chance to get them on board as you move forward. Don't worry about that. First, you must know where you're headed so that you can start making progress towards that vision.

Strategy #35 Like Ross, Learn How to Pivot

The last step is that we have to pivot. And if you're not a *FRIENDS* fan, I'm so sorry that you won't get the joke, but PIVOT! We have to make adjustments. Your vision changes over time.

I make a new vision board every single year. I begin each year with a new, clear vision of what I want in the next five or ten years. So why does it change? Two major reasons: achievement and change. Once you achieve pieces within your vision, that are painted in that picture, you need to now work on something else.

Sometimes as you move forward, you start to see new parts of your vision. You get clearer and more focused. Parts of your vision may drift off and new things may come in your vision. My life's vision at age 20 is not the same as my vision for my life at 38. It's different because I'm different. THANK GOD!

All you need to do is create a vision that captivates you to move forward right now. And three months from now, if you're not feeling it, if you're less captivated, you can revisit the process. Let's recreate that vision now, even though we know we're going to have to make adjustments. Nothing is permanent. For most of us, our work, our lives, our email or notifications, they are not life or death. Paint the vision that you want and adjust as needed.

You're allowed to change your mind.

Let me say that again: you are allowed to change your mind.

When I started my Ph.D. program, I was 100% certain that I wanted to be a community college president, which is why I needed a Ph.D. I mean, I liked school, but another five years of it was not my idea of a great time. But, it was the checkbox I needed to get the job I wanted. So I went for it. Full steam ahead. Then, about three or three and a half years in, I started to have a different vision. I didn't want to be an administrator. I wanted to work directly with the students. Which, technically, I was doing with just a master's degree. It started to become harder to go to class, or to focus on my research, because I just didn't see the degree being necessary to my future. I had changed my mind.

On top of changing my mind, now I was feeling guilty. So I wasn't going to class because I wasn't sure I still wanted it. Then, I was feeling guilty about not going to class. It was a very stressful time for me and my husband, Matt. We had a "come to Jesus" meeting as a family and said, look we are already this far in, let's finish the degree. You can always choose not to use it, but once you have it...you have it.

So, I continued down the path. Finished my research, graduated, and before the ink was dry on my diploma, I quit my job and started my own business. I had changed my mind. My vision had changed. And that was okay. It is not about feeling guilty for making a change. It is about embracing what you truly want in life.

The moral of the story...Don't fall so in love with your vision that you stop asking yourself, *Is this still what I want?* You need to keep asking that question. If the answer is no, you need to make a change.

My goal for you is to get that picture clear for where you are right now and what your five-year or ten-year goal looks like. I want you to get that picture clear so that we can make an action list to get you there.

Checklist for captivating visions—more specific vision

- Define success for yourself
- Track each step of your journey
- Ask yourself a bazillion questions
- "Paint your own picture"
- Know your habits
- Learn how to pivot

CHAPTER 7
OPPORTUNITY-FOCUSED

THE NEXT PILLAR is probably the one that most people struggle with in terms of its relationship to mindset and unstoppable success. In fact, when I was creating this framework to share my journey with others, I also struggled with its inclusion. What I realized during my journey is that the difference between the Stevie I knew as a child and the Stevie I had become as an adult was my willingness to jump on opportunities.

When I was younger, I took all the risks. I was willing to go for anything that would get me closer to that vision. As a child, my dream was to be a professional dancer and then to own a dance studio. At 17 years old, I found an opportunity. A dance studio in need of a manager (who would like to become an owner) in the Australian Outback. I had no idea what the job would entail. I had never been to Australia before. But at the age of 17, I told my parents I was going. I packed up all of my belongings into two suitcases and I left. It was an opportunity, and I took action. It was one of the biggest learning curves of my life, and to this day, I think that experience is what truly led me to become the business owner I am now (even though that venture failed miserably).

Yet, in my 20s I had stopped doing those outrageously, risky things. I had started just walking down the well-traveled path. I started ignoring the opportunities due to fear. As I began my journey to reclaim my name and my life, I realized I would have to take risks. I would have to become that girl who looked at opportunities and went for them. The one who believed that every step forward towards a dream, a vision, was worth it. As much as I hate to admit it, it was tough. As adults, we often let opportunities pass us by because we constantly reevaluate things. We are too stuck in our fear, in our limiting beliefs. But to truly unleash our unstoppable success, we must be willing to stay open and focused on opportunities. We must be willing to take the risks. To step outside of our comfort zone. As I realized this, I realized that this had to be a pillar in the framework.

Being opportunity-focused means we must evaluate opportunities and decide which ones we should take or not take to achieve our success. This involves looking at opportunities through a specific lens to determine how we are going to take action, how we are going to make decisions. Some people call this a decision-making process, and some people call it an action-taking process. No matter what you call it, it's the process you go through personally when you're evaluating whether or not to take an opportunity.

What opportunities have you taken? What opportunities have you let pass you by? I don't believe in opportunity knocking. It's not waiting around for you. If you think about somebody who comes and knocks on your door, they knock and then they wait there for like a minute or two to see if you're home. I don't think opportunity does that for us in business or in life. It doesn't hang around your door hoping that you answer or leave a pamphlet attached like the local lawn service company.

Strategy #36 Recognize the Red Convertible of Opportunity

I think opportunity is a red convertible with the top down. It's cruising down your street just slow enough that if you run and jump, you can be in on the opportunity.

That's opportunity.

It's not knocking at your door waiting for you to open it. It's driving down your street, and you've got to take action. We need to evaluate opportunities. I am always thinking, *How do I take action fast?* Opportunities, like fast cars, don't wait around. We need to jump on them quickly.

There are a few steps that we must go through when looking at our decisions/our opportunities. You're going to feel like you're trudging through to make decisions. Trust me, it gets faster. This is a process. The more you do it, the faster it becomes. It could take you a minute or two to decide on the phone when an opportunity is presented. But I want to make sure that you think through every step of it, because it's going to allow you to choose the best opportunities for you.

What does this look like? Well, it looks like asking yourself a whole lot of questions. That's what evaluation is all about. What would this opportunity give you? Is it something that is going to benefit you personally or professionally? If it's not, I feel like the answer's already there, right? If it's not going to benefit you, why are you even looking at the opportunity?

If it passes the benefit test, cool. Let's look at the benefits of this opportunity. However, we also have to look at the costs. Often when we're evaluating opportunities, we forget to look at the actual cost of that opportunity. It's going to cost you something. It's going to cost you time. It's going to cost you money. It's going to cost you effort. Every opportunity and every decision has a cost. Maybe it's a health cost...taking on that second job means losing some sleep or eating more fast food. What is it going to cost you to take this opportunity? Maybe It's going to cost you a piece of your vision.

Maybe your vision is to always be done with your work at five o'clock. Time to clock out! But maybe taking this opportunity means you're going to work till seven. Well, that's costing you family time and taking away that from your overall vision. You have to decide: I*s that okay? Is the cost worth the opportunity?*

Pardon my language but in this example, if it were my life, that answer is a resounding "Hell no!" In my opinion, the cost of sacrificing family time is too high. It is TOO important to my vision, so if the opportunity means giving up that time, I have to say no. That is my decision, but you will have to make that decision for yourself.

If we think about the Success Model, these are logical thoughts and beliefs. But, how do you feel about the opportunity? Are you excited? Are you scared? Are you nervous? Is it going to push you outside your comfort zone? Does it feel aligned with the vision for your life? If this opportunity, if this red convertible is not heading down the street in the direction you're heading, why are you jumping in? You've got to make sure the opportunity supports your dreams and goals.

There is a point at which an opportunity is outside of your comfort zone, but it goes too far and it goes into the chaos zone. When we think about the comfort zone, I want you to think about a target, a bullseye with circles. The inner circle, the smallest one in the center, is your safety zone. That's where you're not growing. In the inner circle, you're not pushing yourself. Everything is safe. And most of us spend the majority of our time in the safety zone. Which is A-OK, but sometimes we have to step outside and take a risk.

Once you get past that inner circle, the safety zone, you get outside your "comfort zone." Once you get outside that comfort zone, then you're in the growth zone, the second ring. And the growth zone is a great place to be. It allows you to grow, to learn new things, and to step into your greatness. I always encourage my clients to make decisions based on what keeps them in this circle at least 50% of the time. I believe that if you spend time every day, every week growing and learning, you will have a life that truly allows you to step into your greatness.

The problem is that we can go too far. We can step so far outside of our comfort zone that we enter the chaos zone. That's the bigger circle. What I have found in working with my clients is this is where stuff starts to fall apart. They thought the opportunity was good. They thought it was going to do well for them, but it was so far removed from what they knew. It was so far outside their comfort zone that it caused chaos in their lives. They don't know what they're doing. They don't know what they're working on. They don't know where they're headed. We never want to get there if we can help it. While chaos is a part of life, it's not a part we want to bring on ourselves. Let's make sure that the opportunities we're looking at are solidly in the growth zone. Now, maybe that opportunity would send you into chaos right now. That doesn't mean that opportunity might not be in your growth zone a year from now! Look at all of your options and really consider what you are working towards.

I remember working with a client who was looking to sell his business, exit, and go to a new business. But he wasn't ready to do it quite yet. It was in his vision for the next five years, but at that point in time, he wasn't quite ready yet. Then one day, he received an email. Somebody was interested in buying the business, but in order to buy the business, they needed him to do X, Y, and Z with it. They had these conversations and he was excited about the opportunity. But he could tell that if he took the opportunity right away, it was going to cause him chaos. There were so many things he would need to do to be able to take the opportunity that his current business would struggle. And then the investor wouldn't want to buy it.

Since the opportunity felt like it was too far outside his growth zone, he decided to say no to the opportunity at that moment. Two years later, he reached out to that same company and said, *"Hey, I know I said no two years ago, I wasn't ready then. My business is ready now, and I'm ready. Now, if this is still something you'd be interested in bringing under your umbrella, let's have that conversation."* And he was able to sell his company to that original prospect. He knew not to go into the chaos zone, and hopped in the red convertible when he was ready. Had he jumped into that chaos zone, everything might have fallen apart.

We must evaluate these opportunities, not just what they look like on paper, but really explore how they're going to impact our lives as we pursue them.

Let's say you've done the evaluation and your opportunity still looks good. You know this is something you want to do. You know it is in the growth zone. You feel inspired and excited by it.

Now, you're going to go to your belief systems. There are four major beliefs that most people feel get in the way of opportunities.

Strategy #37 Look Fear Directly in the Eyes

The first belief is simple, plain, and standard...fear. *I'm scared to do this. I'm not sure I can do this. I'm feeling some imposter syndrome. What if it goes wrong? What if it leads me the wrong way?*

The root of this is fear of the unknown. You must look at that belief and ask yourself, H*ow will I handle this fear?* If you continue to feel it while you go for this opportunity, you're not going to win. It's not going to work for you because you are resistant to the opportunity due to fear. You have to get unafraid so that you can take the risks. Fear of the unknown is battled by knowledge. So do your research. Focus on learning everything you can so you can take away the unknown and you won't be plagued by this fear.

Another type of fear that people have is fear of success. This occurs when you think to yourself, *If the opportunity works out, if it goes well, I'm going to lose some of my flexibility. I'm going to lose some of my ownership. I'm going to lose some of my family time.* There's a cost associated with success. And that's a really important thing to look at. You're scared of what it will cost you in terms of time, effort, support, finances and health if you say "yes." An example of that is moving up in a job. Whether you are a business owner thinking about taking on a new, bigger client, or whether you're in a job looking to promote to that next level, realistically with more power comes more responsibility.

I remember when I was working in corporate America and wanted to move up to that next level. I had fear of success, knowing if it went well and I landed the job, it meant I would work longer hours. It would cost me some nights and weekends. I really had to evaluate: *is this a good opportunity for me?* And I realized if I took this opportunity that I'd have to reprogram my beliefs around that. Otherwise, that fear would show up as resistance.

Many of us have a fear of judgment. We are worried about what other people will think, what other people will say, and whether other people will judge us if they see us pass up an opportunity. And as we know, people are super judgy! They're going to judge you for everything. If we let ourselves be held back from opportunities because we're afraid of other people's judgment, we're never going to reach the success that we know is possible within us. In order to remove fear of judgement, you have to create a rock-solid belief in yourself that will be stronger and last longer than another's judgement of you.

Last is fear of failure. I think that's one that most people know and have. *What if this fails? What if it doesn't work out? What if I will never be successful? I am going to be responsible for the outcome for my team, whatever it may be, and what if I cause our team to fail?*

Fear of failure is normal and something that we will battle throughout our lives. The only way to overcome the fear of failure is to reframe the idea. Failure is never final. Failure is about learning that it didn't work out this time.

In order to take this opportunity, we've got to identify the beliefs, including the types of fear, that we have. We need to reprogram them into something positive. You've got to do the inner work to figure that out. Start by writing some of them down. Then you can think about reprogramming those beliefs. Remember that our beliefs cause our feelings, our actions, and our results. If we are able to reprogram the beliefs, then we can change the outcomes.

Start saying things like, *This opportunity will cause me to grow.* That's a really good thing! *This opportunity is worth the investment of my time and my money because it's going to get me to that next level. This opportunity will allow me to become the XYZ. The person I've always wanted to be. I will be successful. I will make this work. I will be proud of myself, right?*

What I want you to start thinking about is what beliefs do you have that you need to start reprogramming. You may not have an opportunity sitting in front of you, but that doesn't mean you can't start reprogramming those beliefs.

Let's get rid of fear of failure.

Let's get rid of fear of success.

Let's get rid of fear of judgment.

Let's just get rid of fear.

A little bit of fear is healthy. I mean, I swim with sharks, after all! Let's get rid of all the other fears, the fears that limit us, that hold us back. If we can start reprogramming our brain, when the opportunity shows up, we're more able to say "yes" and make the most of it.

Strategy #38 Remove Attachment to the Outcome

Once you've reprogrammed your beliefs, you have to remove the attachment you have to that outcome. This is not necessarily the easiest one to do. Especially for those of us who are self-proclaimed overachievers. You like to be successful. You have been successful. You are successful, which means removing attachment to the outcome is difficult.

If we're going to evaluate opportunities without beliefs that hold us back, we have to be okay if they don't work out. We can't have an attachment to the outcome. We must say to ourselves, *Whether it works or not has no value or worth declaration on me. I can try this. And you know what? Even if this fails, I'm still good. I'm still worthy. I'm still successful. My value and my worth do not change.*

When we're attached to an outcome, it's like gripping sand. When you grip sand, it starts to flow through your fingers. The tighter you grip it, the more it flows out through your fingers. It's similar to a stress ball. If you grip it too tightly, the ball can pop out of your fingers from the pressure. The more we have our hands grasped on the outcome of that opportunity, the more likely that the opportunity will be squeezed through our fingers.

Instead, we have to hold it gently like a bouncy ball. We just want to hold onto it lightly because we have no attachment to the outcome. Nine times out of ten, with the opportunities that present themselves to us, we actually can't force the outcome. It relies on other people. It relies on timing. It relies on marketing. It relies on strategies. So we can't guarantee the outcome. What we can guarantee is that we have the right mindset and we've removed our attachment to the outcome. We can guarantee, we can control our thoughts, emotions, and behaviors.

Remembering the Success Model, our BEBO model, everything is a circle. Every part of the circle supports the other parts. This is so important because beliefs equal outcomes. If you believe that this opportunity has to be successful, that you cannot afford for it not to be. If that's what you believe, then this may not be the right opportunity for you. We have to remove our attachment to the outcome so that we can truly invest in the opportunity at our highest level. This is the mindset we have to be in before we take opportunities. *If it works awesome; if it doesn't work, I'm still good.*

Strategy #39 Make a Decision

Once you've done all these other steps, you're ready to decide that you're going to take action. You have a decision tree which starts with whether it's a yes and no. If it's a no, let it go. Let the opportunity pass you by. Let that red convertible drive on past your house and wave at the people in it. Wish them the best. Go back inside your house and get to work. It's okay to say no to opportunities even if you're a go-getter. Just because you may be an overachiever doesn't mean you have to say yes to everything. Trust me. This is coming from someone who was a "Yes Woman" for way too long.

Sometimes the decision is a maybe, and that means you need to negotiate some of the factors of that opportunity. These are the opportunities that make you think to yourself, *This may be a good opportunity if X, Y, and Z occur.* Negotiate and ask for what you need. Again, if the opportunity doesn't hit those check boxes, then it's a hell no! It moves to the "no" category. The only reason to put something in "maybe" is you need some clarification. Once you get the clarification, you should be able to make your decision.

Strategy #40 DO IT NOW!

Finally, let's say you have done your evaluation of the opportunity, and it's a "yes." Take action. Go do it. Say yes! Tell the person you're going to do it now.

For many of us, there's still one last step we have to do. We've got to pray. Check in with your gut and then move forward. Many of us need to pray on it. Ask for a sign from the Universe, journal about it, meditate, or set aside some quiet time for yourself to think. If you're talking about a big decision, a big opportunity, you have to really think through it and you might need to sit with it right now.

Check your alignment with your vision. Is this going to get me to my goal? Is this aligned? Is this pushing me forward? Is this where I want to be? And then breathe. Right? Take some deep breaths. Make sure you still feel good about it. Then communicate. The answer is yes to that opportunity.

Warning: Don't sit with it forever. I have found that once you decide that the answer is a "yes," if you don't take action within eight hours, you start talking yourself out of it. Don't pray too long. Don't wait for the Universe for too long. Don't wait for that sign for three weeks. If you've already said "yes," mentally, and you're just wanting one last check-in, give yourself three or four hours. However, you've got to take action within eight or you're going to start talking yourself out of it.

Whoever gave it to you, whatever you're looking at, communicate and take action within eight hours. If you have bought the big expensive car, it seems really cool driving it home. But then some-time overnight is when you start to ask, *"Wow, that was a big invest-ment. That was a lot of money. What if I don't like it as much as I thought?"* So say yes and take action within eight hours, or you might risk going back through the process again because you've sat on it for too long. And if you've decided you need to reevaluate, now you're going to go all the way back through the process. So you want to make sure that you take action quickly so that you can act on that opportunity.

Remember that the red convertible doesn't stop for you! Be ready to hop into its seat by evaluating, reprogramming your beliefs, removing the attachment, and taking action. This is the process we're going to use to evaluate our opportunities, but we have to stay open to them and we have to stay focused on them.

Start working through the process by considering an opportunity that maybe you're currently facing. If you don't have an opportunity right now, but you're thinking right about an opportunity for the future that you might want to do that you might want to take, that's okay. Start working on your beliefs. Start working on removing attachment. You can do that now, even if you don't have an opportunity right in front of you. You will be ready when you hear that red convertible revving up outside.

Here's your checklist for when you hear the engine revving and know the red car is approaching your driveway!

Checklist for reviewing an opportunity

- Evaluate
- Assess the fear
- Remove attachment to the outcome
- Make the final decision
- Write down your affirmation and keep it nearby!

CHAPTER 8
MAGNETIC MINDSET

ONCE THERE WAS a boy who lived with his family on a farm. The boy and his dog would go down to the pond for hours every day in the spring and summer to practice retrieving various items. The boy wanted to prepare his dog for any scenario that may come up during duck season because he wanted his dog to be the best hunting dog in the whole county.

The boy and his dog had vigorous training sessions every day until the dog was so obedient, he wouldn't do anything unless he was told to do so by the boy.

As duck season rolled in with the fall and winter months, the boy and his dog were eager to be at their regular spot down at the pond near their house. Only a few minutes passed before the two heard the first group of ducks flying overhead. The boy slowly raised his gun and shot three times before killing a duck, which landed in the center of the pond.

When the boy signaled his dog to retrieve the duck, the dog charged through the duck blind and bushes toward the pond. However, instead of swimming in the water like he had practiced so many times, the dog walked on the water's surface, retrieved the duck, and returned it to the boy.

The boy was astonished. His dog had an amazing ability to walk on water—it was like magic. The boy knew no one would ever believe this amazing thing that he had just witnessed. He had to get someone else down there to see this incredible phenomenon.

The boy went to a nearby farmer's house and asked if he would hunt with him the next morning. The neighbor agreed, and met up with the boy the following morning at his regular spot by the pond.

The pair patiently waited for a group of ducks to fly overhead, and soon enough, they heard them coming. The boy told the neighbor to go ahead and take a shot, which the neighbor did, killing one duck. Just as the day before, the boy signaled to his dog to fetch the duck. Miraculously, the dog walked on the water again to retrieve the duck.

The boy was bursting with pride and could hardly contain himself when he asked his neighbor, "Did you see that? What do you think?!"

The neighbor responded, "I wasn't going to say anything, but your dog doesn't even know how to swim."

The boy sat in disbelief as his neighbor pointed out a potential flaw of the dog rather than recognizing the fact that what he had just done was a miracle[1].

THE REASON that you have the life you currently have, with the results at whatever level they are currently at, is because that is what you are training yourself to do. Now, that might seem a little harsh, but stick with me.

Over years of human behavior and psychological research, we know that our brain is a very powerful muscle. In fact, it controls everything you do. This means that if you want to achieve certain results in your life, you have to be willing to train your brain to make it happen.

Let's say that you want to make $10K a month in your business. What most people do is start looking to expand their strategies. They think, *I need to put more into marketing. I need to find wealthier clients, I need to get on more sales calls.* These are definitely all actions that might lead to earning $10K a month. But it isn't guaranteed, right? What if the marketing strategies don't work? What if you can't connect with wealthier clients? What if you aren't able to close sales over the phone? Will the strategy alone equal success? NO!

Success is only 10% strategy; the rest is mindset.

And the reason we can't guarantee our results is that we are only focusing on the 10%.

That is why understanding your mindset is so important. Many of my clients come to me focused on only the last two pieces of the BEBO Success Model, behaviors and outcomes. They think, *my outcomes aren't what I want so I must change my behaviors to change my results.* Well, the short answer is yes, if you aren't getting the outcome you want, then we will definitely need to look at behaviors. However, if we stop there, we still can't guarantee success.

I can teach people how to sell over the phone (behavior), but if they lack confidence, my strategies won't help them. I can show people how to prospect for new clients, but if they believe they are bothering people, it won't work. The only way to guarantee success is to work our way all the way back through the model to see what beliefs are causing us to feel a certain way, act a certain way, and therefore achieve a certain set of results. Our brains are wired to prove themselves right. As Henry Ford said, "Whether you believe you can or you can't, you are right."

Some of you may be realizing that you are spending a lot of time taking action and seeing no results. Could it be that the strategy doesn't work? Sure. You may be thinking, *But it works for other people, doesn't it? Why doesn't it work for me?* It does not work for you because you don't believe in yourself.

When I share my story of entrepreneurship and I tell people that I went from making $0 in my first year to making $17K in year two to making $158K in year three, people assume that I did something different between year two and year three. They are shocked to hear that it wasn't better marketing or a new Facebook ads strategy I implemented.

What changed between year two and year three was me.

I became more confident, I believed in myself. I had no additional meetings or events in year three than I did in the previous year. I had no bigger audience. But when I got on those sales calls, I believed in myself. I knew that I could solve my potential clients' problems. That belief led me to feel confident. That confidence supported my sales strategy, which led to my success.

What is holding you back from success? What mindset shifts do you need to make? What is this lack of belief currently costing you? Our mindset costs us a lot. It is priceless really, so investing it will always pay off. Without the proper mindset, you are losing. You are losing money, clients, and even more faith in yourself. That's a pretty high price to pay.

Picture this: A young girl, about 5 years old, cuts down her mom's drapes and ties them around her neck. She steps out onto the front porch. There is a light breeze and plenty of sunshine. She climbs up on the railing and looks out over the vast horizon. At that moment, as she puts her arms back and tilts her chin forward...she is not thinking about the potential broken arm, the fact that those rose bushes will hurt, or that she is definitely going to get a whoopin' from her mom when she sees the drapes. The only thing she is thinking is, *What if I really can fly?*

Strategy #41 Understand Your Brain

As children, we always think about the impossible. We live through our imagination. Yet, as we get older, we live based on our past experiences. Basically, we have lived life, and so our brain uses those past experiences to show us what we should do or more often, not do. The power of our brain is amazing. There are two major points about our brains that we must understand in order to train it to work for us.

1. Our brains are wired to protect us. Your brain is designed to keep you safe. It will try to keep you from making mistakes that you have made before. It will try to show you the potential dangers for what you are thinking about. All in an effort to protect you, and yet, it means that most of us stay in our comfort zone.
2. What your brain focuses on, expands. In other words, whatever you look at and focus on, whatever you think about, your brain will try to show it to you.

Let's dive in a little deeper on these two ideas. If your brain is wired to protect you, how do you get out of your comfort zone? First, you have to remember that you are in control, you get to focus on whatever you want. You are in the driver's seat for your brain. SO, what do you want to do? Our past experiences are just that—they are the past. They are what we did before. That doesn't mean we need those experiences to dictate what we do in the present or in the future. Use those past experiences and reminders to increase your knowledge and understanding. Then, take control and move forward. Again, the older we get, the more experiences we have had, which means our brain has more interesting stories and potential warnings to show us. Cool. Listen to them. See them. And then make a conscious decision to do what serves you and your future vision.

I remember several years ago; my husband and I were looking to buy a new car. I really wanted to test-drive a Chevy Malibu. Mostly because a friend of mine has one and it looked pretty. As soon as we started to have this conversation about a new car, the weirdest thing happened. I started to notice Malibus at every stoplight. I would go to the grocery store and there would be five Malibus in the parking lot. Now, I had to ask myself, was it that there were more Malibus on the road today than there were last week? Nope. The only thing that changed is that I had told my brain to focus on it. It became something that I wanted to see, and so my brain showed it to me.

That's what our brains do for us. We are pummeled with messages and visual stimulation all day long. We can't possibly take it all in, so our brain picks the pieces that it feels are important to our current focus and that is what it brings to light.

This of course begs the question...what are you focusing on? Often, we find ourselves focusing on the things we don't want! We worry about the future. We replay past conversations with our boss. We are anxious about that pitch next week. We start asking ourselves, *What's the worst thing that can happen?* And our brain answers the question. Our brain, in wanting to dutifully answer our question, starts showing us all the BAD things that could happen. As a result, we get more and more anxious. Suddenly everything we are focusing on is negative. We are training our brains to show us all of those results, to PROVE us right that everything will go WRONG!

We are addicted to our thoughts and decisions that are based on our past. Why? It is because the brain stores all you do and say. Yikes!

The brain and mind are always providing you with what you are focusing on. When it comes to success, it's really important to be able to see the positive outcomes. We must ask ourselves, *what is the best thing that could happen?* When we start focusing on the positive our brains start showing us the possibilities. You need to ask, *What is possible in my business? Where do I REALLY want to go?* And to be honest, we aren't good at asking these questions.

We have to be willing to ask the impossible questions and believe impossible things. Easier said than done, I know. Why is this so difficult for us? The truth is that somewhere along the path to becoming an adult you were told to pay your bills, wash your face, stop believing in Santa Claus, and plan for the worst.

Think about that for a second. When did that become the best approach? Always thinking about the worst possible scenario? Are you focusing on the dog that can't swim instead of the dog that can walk on water?

If we want to achieve big things, we have to be willing to ask big questions, and we have to remove the biggest obstacle that stands in our way.

By the way, if you are wondering what the biggest obstacle is…I am here to tell you that you live with it every day and already know it well.

Your biggest obstacle is YOU.

Your thoughts.

Your beliefs.

Your past.

Your story.

Let's talk about story for a moment. If I were to ask you to tell your story, what would you focus on? Think about it. Would it be a story of triumph over adversity? Would you focus on what you don't have? Would you focus on how far you've come?

One of the questions we are asked on a seemingly daily basis is, "tell me a little about yourself." What do you say? Are you talking with others about your business with a bright focus on the future? Or do you talk more about what you wish was happening? Is your story that business is great and getting better or are you saying that business could be better. Do you see the difference? It is small but mighty. When we talk about ourselves in an interview, we focus on the positive and tend to focus on family and educational background. Cool, but that is not your whole story. What is your whole story? If someone were to write your autobiography what would you include? What would you conveniently forget? What would you skip over?

When I work with clients, we spend the first few sessions talking about their story. Your history does NOT dictate your future. However, most of us let it. We often let our past dictate what we can accomplish in our future. We tell ourselves, *I failed on that last call so I will fail at this one.* We don't allow ourselves to improve. We assume that whatever happened before will repeat itself. Well, if you focus on it, it sure will repeat. You have to be able to look at your past for what it taught you. Your past is a growth plan, not a map. It is not showing you what will happen. Your story shows you what you have survived, what you have grown through, what you have learned.

Your story is a teacher, not a fortune-teller.

Ask yourself: Where in your life are you letting the past dictate your future? Where are you allowing your story to be set on repeat?

Strategy #42 Write Your Own Story

The first step to owning your story is being able to know what it is. Identify and overcome. Learn and leverage. If you want to create a successful life for yourself, you have to be able to let go of the past, and use it correctly, as a launchpad for your future.

One of the best ways to identify your story is to create a timeline. Take out a sheet of paper and draw a line across it. On the far left side, the day you were born. On the far right of the page, today. Now, I want you to record all the moments you can remember between those two points. What experiences stand out in your life? What experiences are easy to recall? Good memories. Bad memories. Put them all down there. Large moments and small things are both welcome. It is important to just start recording the history of YOU. Anything you can remember is good.

Once you have written down everything you can think of, take a step back and just look at your life. Revel in all that you have overcome. Everything that you have learned. Once you can identify the history, the past that you have lived, you can then focus on how to make sure your future is written by you.

Some of you may be saying, *"This is great, Stevie Dawn, but so what? How does this help me push forward?"*

Well, you have to take action. While we are talking all about the brain and getting your mind right, it doesn't mean that you can just sit back and wait for your brain to shape up. Nope, not happening. You have to take action. You have to start training your brain. How are you taking control of your future? How are you moving yourself forward by telling your brain what you want it to show you? What do you want it to focus on?

Strategy #43 Stop If/Then Living

When we talk about mindset shifts, there are lots of different ways to get there…and we have discussed a number of them in this book. You can meditate. You can journal. You can develop mantras and a vision board. All of these are good options, but they involve taking action.

Action is not about getting ready to get ready. It is not living an "IF/THEN" life.

In my late 20s I was stuck in the "IF/THEN" life. IF this comes through, THEN I can achieve that. If I get this deal then I can celebrate (instead of celebrating the fact that I did the work). We focus our "if" statements on outcomes. Remember just one chapter ago, we talked about having no attachment to the outcomes. The thing about all the "ifs" is that they create this idea that we aren't in control. That we have to be waiting for something or someone else to come along and give us what we need. Of course, there are moments where the IF/THEN is true within our lives, but we need to be in control. We need to focus on what we are doing to make things happen. WHEN I do this, I WILL receive that.

We have to stop waiting. Stop getting ready to get ready. If you are familiar with the musical *Hamilton*...we must be a Hamilton instead of a Burr. (If you haven't seen the movie, check it out and be inspired as I was!)

Strategy #44 Get into Your Own "Shark Cage"

As you have learned at the start of this book, I love sharks. In fact, I have a t-shirt that says, "The Great White Is My Patronus" (Potterhead, anyone?). I really believe it to be true. The great white gives me strength, hope and courage. Now, I understand that sharks are not everyone's favorite animal. I started out scared to death to go in the ocean because my parents allowed me to watch the movie *Jaws* when I was 4 years old. No judgment on my parents, please, but really?! Later in life, I got over it. I became a fanatic. Heck, I even won the Shark Week sweepstakes for an all-expenses-paid trip to cage dive with great whites off the coast of Mexico.

(Fun story: While watching Shark Week, I tweeted my favorite type of shark. Of course said, "Great Whites, all the way!" and promptly went to bed. I awoke the next morning to find my Facebook and Twitter accounts had exploded, telling me that I had won the Shark Week sweepstakes for a five day, fully paid, fully inclusive vacation to go cage diving with Great White sharks off the coast of Mexico at Guadalupe Island. Amazing! That's how I had the trip of a lifetime.)

Cage diving was an incredible experience for all kinds of reasons, but one of the first experiences was the most memorable. We got up on the second morning and it was time to get in the cage. They have you sit on the edge of the boat, right above the cage and put on a weighted vest and a regulator (which is an oxygen hose attached to the boat) so you can stay underwater. Then you are supposed to lower yourself down into the cage while breathing slowly.

Normal breathing? Yeah, I am not breathing normally while I am seeing these 12-foot creatures gliding by. It is not really a "breathe easy" kind of moment, even for a shark fangirl such as myself!

What did I do? I keep thinking about it...*breathe...breathe...*which made my mind do what? Keep breathing faster to the point that by the time I started to climb down the ladder, I was hyperventilating. I was getting ready to get ready. I was so focused on making sure I was breathing, I had stopped being able to breathe. The power of our brains, am I right?! I was taking my time preparing instead of just jumping in and letting my lungs do what they know how to do. I was forcing my brain into anxiety just by thinking the word *breathe*!

From then after when it was my turn in the cage, I just put the regulator in and went down. No thinking, no preparation. And I was breathing just fine.

I learned a lot of things about sharks that I can relate to life. One lesson speaks to taking action. What did I learn? If you spend all your time getting ready to get ready, you will never make it into the cage. If you spend all your time thinking about taking action but never doing it, you will be frustrated and stuck in your life.

What can you take action on today? What can you focus your brain on? When we put the power of our brains to work for our positive outcomes, the world shifts and amazing things can happen.

Checklist for having a magnetic mindset

- Understand your brain
- Write your own story
- Stop if/then living
- Get into your own "shark cage"

CHAPTER 9

ELEVATED HABITS

Do you set New Year's resolutions? Some people do, some people don't, and I have no judgment here either way.

I used to set a lot of New Year's resolutions, but it always seemed like they didn't come true. That happens to many of us. Our New Year's resolutions don't come to fruition because of two major reasons.

The first reason that New Year's resolutions don't work out is that they are too vague.

Let's say on January 1st, you declare, *"I am going to eat healthier."* That sounds like a noble goal. However, if you set a goal of eating healthier, well, what does eating healthier really mean? I mean, does it mean I have to eat only plant-based food and become a vegetarian? That's one way to eat healthier. Or, instead of ordering pizza twice a week, you will only order it once a week?

Eating healthier is really important for how we behave and feel. If you make the goal too vague, it's really hard to know if you achieve that goal or not. And you can become frustrated and start ordering pizza three times a week.

The second way we set New Year's resolutions that can lead us astray is if we make them too specific. If you make a resolution that is so flipping specific it's hard to achieve, you set yourself up for failure. For example, let's say you're trying to lose weight and you decide that you're going to set a goal of losing 25 pounds. Anybody who's tried to lose weight before will tell you that trying to hit a specific number can be really hard.

Sometimes you drop 30 pounds, but then you gain seven pounds. Your weight shifts and it changes. Can you really hit the 25-pound mark and keep it consistently? Probably not. And when you don't hit that goal weight, you feel bad. You feel guilty. Sometimes, people try really hard and do all the right things to lose weight, but still can't. They give up.

One of the things I learned years ago, and now it has become just the backbone of my business and in my life, is that it's not about setting goals. It's about creating habits. In the end, what stops us from achieving, whether it be a New Year's resolution or any other goal we might set, what gets in our way is us. And the fact that we don't have habits that support us.

Why are habits or routines important? Habits are what allow our brains to go on autopilot. By utilizing habits, we can focus on processing the harder decisions, the harder problems, and solutions we need to give our brain time to ponder.

Have you ever had one of those situations where you get up, you get ready, and you head to work. You drive to work and a co-worker asks, *"How was the traffic?"* And you say, *"Was there traffic? I don't remember. I don't really remember driving here this morning."* I know it's happened to me a bunch of times. Driving to work is a habit and our muscle memory takes over. We can actually get to work and not remember the drive. Now, that is just a tad bit scary because we are driving a motor vehicle. That's not the safest way to do it, but hey, that's our brain at work. Many of us have probably had amazing thoughts, solutions, and ideas while we're driving (or maybe in the shower?). And it's because your brain goes on autopilot and that frees your mind to think about these ideas. Habits are muscle memory. And when you turn on that memory, your brain goes into autopilot and you can start thinking about other things.

Habits are important because they give us thinking time. But the other reason habits are important is because they predict our outcomes.

"We are what we repeatedly do.
Excellence, then, is not an act, but a habit." — Will Durant

The truth is that for most of us, our habits are what lead us to success or what gets in the way of our success. Once again, we use the Success Model, that says beliefs activate emotions, emotions, influence behaviors, behaviors, dictate outcomes, and outcomes reinforce beliefs. We're focused on this behavior circle because this is where our habits and our routines exist. This is what dictates our outcomes. We can have great thoughts. We can have our emotions in line, but if we're doing the wrong habits or we're not doing the habits we need to do at all, we're not going to have the results we want. We're not going to have the outcome.

When I'm working with a client, we work backwards. We look at the outcome that isn't working. We say, *"That isn't what you want."* And we start tracing it backward. *"Why is that outcome happening?"* One of the first questions that I ask people is, *"What are your habits? What are the things that you're doing? Are they working for you? Are they working against you?"* Once we identify the behaviors and the habits that are leading to the outcomes, the good news is we can change those. Everything within this model is within our control. If we set a goal and then we work backwards, we can see which habits and behaviors we need to do so that we can consistently hit that goal.

We are what we repeatedly do. Which for me begs the question: *Who are you?* Habits not only lead us to our outcomes, they not only allow our brain to process, they are also how we define ourselves and how we define others. I want you to take a second here and think.

When you do what you do repeatedly, what or who are you?

If an outsider was to look at your life, to look at the things that you do every day, to look at the things you do every week, every month, how would they define you? What label would they give to you? I want you to think about that.

If you show up late to work every day, you're a late person. You're a tardy person, maybe an unreliable person.

If you show up every day and you make a to-do list and then you cross it off, you're an achiever. You're a go-getter. You're a "get shit done" person.

If you always put other people first, always care about others first, and we see that in your actions and your habits, your behaviors, your caregiver, you're empathetic. You're kind.

What are you doing every day? And how is that defining your life?

Are you a coffee drinker? Heck, I do that every day. So that is part of who I am. I am a coffee drinker.

Maybe you're a caregiver. Maybe you're a go-getter. A goal-setter. Maybe you're a runner. Maybe you're a CrossFit person. Maybe you're a healthy eater.

What are you?

You could define yourself by titles. I'm a mom, I'm a daughter. I'm a friend. I'm a lover. I'm a spouse. I'm a wife. But what if we actually looked at how your habits work? What would you say about yourself? Are you a procrastinator? Are you lazy? Are you lacking?

We can define ourselves by our habits. both what we do and what we don't do. When we're talking about goals that we want to achieve, I'm going to challenge you to look at what you're doing every day.

Strategy #45 Define Your Habits

Take out a sheet of paper and start defining yourself by your habits. Examine what you do every day. From the time you get out of bed to the time you go to bed. Actually, those are habits, too. When do you get up? When do you go to bed? Habits can be things you do every day, or if we get even more granular, they can be things we do monthly, quarterly, or yearly. But what are the habits? Make a list.

The next step is to go through the list you made and ask yourself the question: Does this habit support my goals? Will it get me closer to that vision I have in my head? My dream? My success?

When you start making this list of your habits, you may find things you don't like. That's okay. That awareness is going to lead you to making and breaking habits. We have to start somewhere. And I want you to start by really thinking about identifying these habits for yourself and identifying where you are.

The Ugly Truth

Okay, here is the ugly truth. If I'm 100% honest, the truth is that we don't analyze our habits very often. In fact, most of us have habits that we do every day and have never analyzed. We've never examined them to see if they're serving us.

Perhaps they're bad. Perhaps they're slowing us down. Perhaps they're hurting our relationships and we never realized it.

The first thing we have to do is to understand what our habits are. What are you doing repeatedly every day, every week, every month? That is your first action item is to identify your habits. Now, I want to pause here to make a pretty bold statement.

The biggest obstacle to achieving any goal is ourselves.

We are the only reason we don't achieve goals. We don't set ourselves up for success. Many of us blame other people. We can point a lot of fingers, but at the end of the day, we are the ones who get in the way of us achieving goals.

How are you going to start getting out of your own way?

The answer is you start changing some habits. Once you know what you are doing, you can start identifying two different categories. What you aren't doing and what you are doing that you really shouldn't be doing. Let's be honest, we are all guilty of having bad habits. The habits that don't serve us.

Strategy #46 Identify Your Triggers

What makes and breaks our habits are triggers. There are psychological triggers. There are trauma triggers. There are triggers for everything because triggers are actually what caused us to do the habits.

Think of it this way, you have a habit of getting up every day at 7 a.m. Why? What is the trigger?

Triggers can be anything. They can be processes. You do step one and then you automatically do steps two, three, and four. They can be places, people, things, songs, phrases, ideas, and emotions.

What triggers you to wake up in the morning? An alarm clock? Your phone? You are triggered to wake up because the alarm goes off. That is the trigger to the habit.

What triggers the student to pack up their backpack before class is over? Is it the time pressure to move to another class?

What triggers you to make dinner? Likely, it's because you're at home and you're hungry. Or, if you're like me and keep a consistent schedule, it is 5:30 pm and you make dinner because 5:30 is time for dinner.

There are triggers for everything, good and bad. Once you identify these triggers, you can create change—or stop them—to benefit you and your success.

My client Nancy is somebody who gets overwhelmed a lot. In fact, I would say that overwhelm is her habit. It's an emotional habit. When she came to work with me, we looked at why she was getting overwhelmed. We realized the trigger for her overwhelm was checking her email on her phone. Nancy would be lying in bed. Her alarm would go off, she would pick up the phone and she would start seeing the emails. The emails were the trigger that caused her to become overwhelmed. The overwhelm would continue throughout the day because she would constantly receive emails. Nancy felt overwhelmed because she felt like she could never catch up.

We identified her trigger, and now she was aware that the trigger for her overwhelm was checking the email on the phone. Step number one, let's stop looking at our email on our phone while we're still in bed. We haven't gotten up yet. Let's not start work during the first ten seconds with our eyes open by immediately addressing emails. Let's do something else.

Step number two for Nancy was to look at how she organizes and filters her email. We decided to reduce the number of emails she receives. By adding a filter, Nancy received a smaller number of emails.

The last thing in terms of triggering this overwhelm came from a very specific question I asked Nancy. I asked, *"What is it about email on your phone that gets you to that feeling? Is it that you have 20 emails? Is it that you have 2000 emails? Is there a certain number?"*

Nancy thought about it, and said, *"I feel overwhelmed when I have to scroll."* If there were enough emails that she had to scroll through to see all of the news emails, that was the point where she felt overwhelmed. We asked together, *"What can we do to stop that trigger?"* Well, after ceasing to look at her phone first thing in the morning and organizing her email more effectively, the answer was for Nancy to open email on her computer. Why? She could fit more messages on her computer screen than on her much smaller phone screen. As a result, when Nancy looks at her emails on the computer, she doesn't have to scroll as much. And she doesn't feel as overwhelmed.

What I told Nancy is the first time she checks email to check it on a computer, and not on her phone. Just changing that trigger, and creating a new habit, made her feel less overwhelmed. Her habits are now supporting her peace, her calm, and her success instead of just supporting the overwhelm.

Therefore, in order to break a habit, change the trigger.

Let me give you another example. I am a procrastinator. And I procrastinate for two major reasons. Number one, if I don't like the tasks, I don't want to do them. I hate doing chores around the house. I don't want to dust. I don't want to vacuum. So I procrastinate until my house is so filthy that I feel forced to either clean or move. Am I the only one who has ever considered moving instead of cleaning house? UGH!

The other reason I procrastinate is because I tell myself I work better under pressure. Since I have the belief that with my procrastination I work better under pressure, I would delay doing things till the last minute. So, if I wanted to change that habit, I had to establish pressure for myself.

How I addressed this was by changing my deadlines. I decided any client work for next week that's due must be completed by Friday at five. I must have all client work completed for next week. Now, is that true? Well, I mean, if I'm not meeting with somebody until Thursday, I probably have time Monday, Tuesday, and Wednesday to do it. But the point is that I know that I work better under pressure. When I move up that deadline, I create pressure for myself. Setting those deadlines only works if you work well under pressure, and if you hold yourself accountable.

Quick aside: Why is it so important to hold yourself accountable? You are the most important relationship you have in your life. Let's face it, you are stuck with you for the rest of your life, for however long that is. Most of us wouldn't break promises to other people. Why, then, would you think that it's okay for you to break promises to yourself? The reason many people have accountability partners is because they don't want to break promises to them, but they are willing to break promises to themselves.

Returning to my Friday at five deadlines, are they fake? Absolutely. I made the deadline earlier than it actually is. But I know I'm not going to break promises to myself because I have to deal with myself every day! Think of holding yourself accountable as keeping promises to yourself. Don't break those promises and you will start impacting your success at a deeper level.

If you truly want to change your habits, you have to start changing the triggers because that's going to get you to success. Too often, triggers send us down the wrong path because we're so programmed into our old routine. If you identify the habits you have, then you start working backward and find those triggers. Once you do, you can take back control. Once you change the trigger you can change the habit. Or, if you need to create a new habit, you can create a trigger for that habit.

Habits are in your control and they can be anything. You can make a trigger out of anything. Often, triggers come before the habit. But there are also times where your triggers may be rewards that come after the habit. *If I do this habit, it gets me this reward.* A reward is also a trigger. It just comes after the habit.

Triggers can be reminders. They can be the first step of a process. They can be a song that you always play when you need to write hard emails, the podcast you always listen to which inspires you in the morning. Any of those are triggers, and trust me, they are customizable. You can create triggers that are not for anybody else, just for you.

When I need to write a document, I always watch the epic *Hobbit* and *Lord of the Rings* movies. For some reason, I have created the trigger that when the Hobbit movie is on, I should be writing. It serves me well. If I need to go to sleep, I listen to classical ballet music. When I need to be inspired, I go to places that I know will inspire me. When I need to get stuff done on a to-do list, I make myself a fresh cup of coffee. In my mind, when I have fresh coffee in my hand, it is time to get to work.

You can create triggers around anything. It's about being thoughtful, intentional, and consistent. At the end of the day, you truly can trigger your greatness. And that's what I want you to focus on.

Strategy #47 Break Up with a Habit

In looking at the list you created of all your habits, I want you to pick one that you want to change. We all have habits we know that we need to break. Work backwards and identify the trigger. I challenge you to change the trigger or stop the trigger. I want you to change it to something more positive. You might be asking, *Stevie Dawn, how long will this take?* It's really not about 24 days, or 21 days, or 90 days to make a habit. That's not it. It's about how quickly you can change the trigger. If you change the trigger, you can change the habit tomorrow.

Stop breaking promises to yourself. Commit to changing the trigger. Once you do change one, pick another habit. Start again. If you have a list of habits you want to start right, then do those.

We have to see that our habits have to align with our goals. If you show up late to work every day, you're not going to get a promotion. If you never follow through on projects, you're not being a caring, compassionate person. If you're scared to make phone calls, you're not going to be able to make sales in your business. So, whatever those triggers, whatever those habits, we've got to take control of them to achieve the success we want.

Strategy #48 Turn Down the Friction

Friction is what occurs when we don't want to do something. When it feels off, bad, or wrong. Friction is really interesting! It could be called resistance. I like to call it friction just to keep it a little different. And come on, it makes you laugh a little, right?! If we add friction on the bad habits side, we're less likely to do it. On the flip side, if we reduce friction on the good habits side, we're more likely to do it.

A study was done years ago, and it was proven that if your gym is over five miles from your home, you are 80% less likely to use it. [12]You're 80% less likely to use it because there is too much friction...getting into your car, driving through all the stoplights, and making the effort.

Studies have also been done about food "nudges," effective little interventions that change habits. Another example is a wellness study at a big conference. Wondering what their participants chose when it came to eating healthy, they set up a breakfast buffet. In addition to a pastry table with muffins and bread, they set up a hot food table with eggs, bacon, and sausage. In addition, they had a third table with fresh fruits and juice. What the conference planners noticed is nobody ended up taking the fruit. When they asked themselves why, they realized it was because people would have to go to extra effort. There was more friction to walk over to the third table. The participants were thinking, *Okay, well, I already got my pastries and my plate's already full. Why go over and get the fruit?* The conference planners reduced the friction. They removed the third table and moved the fruit directly in the middle of the pastry table. So as the participants moved down the buffet line, they thought, *Here's a muffin. Here's a bagel. Oh, let me have a banana. Here's a roll.* The planners found all the fruit would go so fast from the new table that they could barely keep it filled. They were running out of fruit because they reduced friction.

Have you ever heard that in order to make yourself work out, you should put on the clothes or have the clothes nearby? Throughout the year 2020, I basically lived in yoga pants due to the pandemic. Did that mean I worked out? No, no, it didn't. Wearing yoga pants did not equal working out for me. For me, putting on clothes is not the trigger I need to work out. I needed a reward for working out. And once I put a reward attached, that worked. But for you, maybe putting on the clothes will make you work out. I know my husband was a runner for decades and he would sleep in his running shorts and his running shirts. In the morning, all he had to do was put on shoes! Reducing friction to change the triggers, to get you to go, is a personal decision. Start reducing friction where you want to succeed in if there are habits you want to stop or break, and learn what works best for you.

And add friction for yourself where needed. For example, if I want to stop eating a whole pan of brownies, let me start by not buying brownie mix at the store. Now, there's increased friction. If I want brownies, I have to get in my car. I have to drive to the store. I have to buy the brownies. I have to go home. I have to bake. And then I get to eat them! Friction can help us with those triggers for those habits, so use it to your advantage.

The final piece of the habit puzzle is accountability. We all need to be accountable for keeping our habits. This is what will allow us to achieve success. Now, as I already mentioned earlier, personal accountability is incredibly important. Stop breaking those promises to yourself!

Of equal importance is your accountability to others. Find someone you trust and tell them what your habits are going to be. Ask them to help hold you accountable. Knowing that somebody else is holding us accountable is what makes us achieve those goals. For me, I look to my coach for accountability. I tell her I'm going to do something. She calls to make sure I do it.

Now you know that you are what you repeatedly do and that habits are important. We talked about having habit goals, as opposed to just setting up goals that maybe are too vague or too specific and are going to hold us back. We talked about the need to look at our triggers, and that lots of different things can serve as triggers, and how you want to trigger your habits. And then we talked about identifying your habits, shifting your triggers, utilizing friction, and establishing accountability.

What would it feel like if every day you woke up knowing that everything you did that day was taking you one step closer to your goal. How would that feel?

You are the biggest obstacle to that. Once you're aware of that, you can start right away. You must choose to analyze your habits, adapt those triggers, and set yourself up with some accountability. If you do those things today, you can start feeling this way tomorrow because you can start changing your habits. It's not easy, but it is simple. So don't over-complicate it, don't make it a bigger thing than it needs to be. Choose a habit, change it up, get to where you want to go. That's it.

Strategy #49 Take Messy Action

I've been a perfectionist my entire life. That's probably not going to change, even though I know it's not great for me. Because I'm a perfectionist, it means that I tend not to hit the "go" button until I am 100% sure. The problem with that is sometimes that means I never press the "go" button. Many of us have been unwilling to take action because we're just not sure. And that can hold us back.

We have to take messy action. As humans, we actually forgive a lot. Somebody has a typo, somebody misspells the name. No big deal. As long as they don't do it every single day, you pretty much forgive them. You think, *It must've been a bad day,* and you let it pass. While that's not true for everyone, it's true for a lot of people.

If we know that humans are going to make errors, and if we know that we're going to be forgiving when they do, why not allow ourselves to make errors and be forgiving of ourselves? When we look at it this way, we see that taking messy action is saying, *Hey, done is better than perfect because the truth is never going to be perfect.*

As you start elevating your habits, you might encounter your own struggle with perfectionism. You might find yourself not sticking with a habit or giving up quickly, because it isn't perfect. Change is messy. You have to give it the grace and patience to be messy.

When you take action, there are always going to be things you could tweak. After you hit the "go" button, your brain is going to come up with eighteen different ways you could have done it. But if you waited to decide which of those eighteen ways was the best, you might've missed a golden opportunity. You might have never "triggered" the habit.

Sometimes, the mess is where the success is because we know we need to be messy. We need to be willing to put ourselves out there, even if it's not all figured out yet. We need to take the leap and then figure it out along the way.

We won't keep it messy! Heck no. We will make it more organized. We will make it more beautiful. We will do all that on our way. But the first step is to just get out there.

Recently, I wanted to get postcards done for our new musical theater. Our performance is coming up in a few months. There's a little place where you can advertise different upcoming productions. I thought, *You know what? I want to get these dropped off at this place in time before the production. 'Cause I'm not sure when I'll be back in this area.* And so I quickly did them.

I quickly created the postcards, for *Tick, Tick...BOOM!*. I showed them to my husband. I'm so excited because I got them done and they're here and we're good to go.

And he says, *"Those are super cool. One thing I noticed though is there's no contact information on the postcards. There's a QR code for them to buy tickets, but no information to contact us otherwise."* And I was like, "Oh no, I can't believe I forgot that." Something that seems really easy like adding our contact info, and something we should do to answer questions. But the postcards were ready. I could have panicked, hurriedly reprinting the cards. Or I could have said, *"Ugh, these are completely WRONG!"*

You know what I did instead? I printed out a little mailing label with contact information. I stuck it on the back of each postcard, I took them to the theater and I dropped them off. The perfectionist in me wanted to throw them in the trash and make all new ones. But the point was the announcement was time-sensitive, the cards needed to be shared, and people took the cards. I know because I spied on some and saw them walk away with them from the theater.

Another recent example was when I pressed the "go" button on a GoFundMe fundraiser for these musical theater dreams that I have in my heart. I needed to get the message out there, and I needed help and support. And I kept going back and forth on how best to raise the funds. *What's the best way? What will people think?* I realized at the end of the day, I just had to press "go" and figure it out as I went along. I took action.

I think what happens to some of us when we are these perfectionists is we hold back from taking action because we're so scared of what may happen if it's not right. Here's the thing. If nobody donates to my fundraiser, I'll be okay. I'll be okay. It's going to be fine. We still have other options. This is just one little sliver of an idea of fundraising. We can do 10 million other things. But the point is, if I never push the "go" button, if I never put it out there, nobody could ever donate because I would've had no donate button.

Think about what you're holding back on. What have you been unwilling to push the play button on because you're scared? What's made you afraid that it's not going to be an epic success? What do you need to push "play" on so that you take messy action and fix it as you go? You know, the best movie moments are the mistakes. This is the gag reel that they kept in the movie because it is so funny. Those are sometimes the best parts we can have.

Don't worry so much about being perfect. Worry about getting your message out there. Worry about putting yourself out there. Take messy action and find success in the mess. Our habits can be fine-tuned over time. Right now, it is just about taking action to elevate our habits and elevate our success.

Summary of the Six Pillars

1. Bold Confidence
2. Elevated Habits
3. Captivating Vision
4. Opportunity-Focused
5. Magnetic Mindset
6. Emotional Resilience

Bold Confidence

Everything comes down to confidence and knowing where to find it and how to grow it are some of the most impactful skills one can possess.

Elevated Habits

Elevated habits lead to elevated results and create true growth and joy in our lives.

Captivating Vision

When your vision is so compelling and so aligned with your soul that you cannot help but to take a step towards it…that is when success becomes within reach.

Opportunity-Focused

When you become opportunity-focused, you take steps towards opportunities just to see where they go. Knowing that they may not work out but that the journey is much more important than the destination.

Magnetic Mindset

Using a magnetic mindset, you can design and create the life that you want. You can make the things you imagine become reality. You, my dear, can change the world.

Emotional Resilience

When you learn how to become aware of your emotions and how to use them to bounce back from tough situations, you will be unstoppable.

Now that we've reviewed the six pillars, I want you to think back to the introduction. I shared with you, dear reader:

Becoming Stevie Dawn meant learning to always be the shark.

Creating these six pillars is my gift to you! Notice that the first letter in each word of the pillars spells out a word:

BECOME.

Who do you need to BECOME?

What does "becoming" mean to you?

It's time for you to use these six pillars so you can always be the shark in your life.

Checklist for elevating your habits

- Define your habits
- Know that your biggest obstacle is yourself
- Identify your triggers
- Break up with bad habits
- Turn down the friction
- Take messy action
- Remember the six pillars of unstoppable success:

1. Bold Confidence
2. Elevated Habits
3. Captivating Vision
4. Opportunity-Focused
5. Magnetic Mindset
6. Emotional Resilience

CHAPTER 10
UNSTOPPABLE SUCCESS

I ONCE HEARD someone say that our lives are not about moving forward, but rather reclaiming who we truly are.

She was born on March 24th, on a Wednesday in the afternoon. She was perfect as she was. A small, crying human. As a child, she was fearless, brave, and funny. Always the life of the party and never willing to back down from a challenge. She dressed differently, had unique haircuts, and loved to dance. She embodied joy every day. She would often be told that she was "unique, an overachiever, an old soul." She embraced these words without letting them define her. She lived life on her own rules.

Over the last two decades, I have been working to reclaim her. To find my way back to that spirit. Is the journey over: hell no! It is just beginning, but here is where I am now:

I never back down from a challenge.
I am the life of every party.
I dress in a way that makes me feel special.
I dance.
I am brave.

I am fearless.

I am perfect as I am.

My life defies my expectations.

At the end of the day, the number one thing that stops us from having everything we want is ourselves. The way we see ourselves. The way we limit ourselves.

Strategy #50 Take Out Your "Head Trash"

A concept I had to embrace along my journey was the concept of "head trash." Head trash is all the negative thoughts you have about yourself. Sometimes, they are of your own making. Sometimes, they are something someone else said to you, oh so long ago. Old relationship scars that haven't healed and it all becomes garbage filling up our brains. It is trash that takes up valuable space in your head (and in your heart).

We've got to clear out the trash so we can get our brain focused on the right things. We've got to take out the trash.

First, write down all the negative stuff. All the things you think others think of you. All the things people expect of you. Write 'em all down. Make a big long list. No judgement. This might be a page long and it might be 10 pages long. Do not judge yourself. Just get all the trash out of your head. Then, crumple it up and throw it away. Or, if you are feeling really spicy, burn it.

You have to take out the trash to clear the way for better thoughts and better results.

I remember when I did this the first time, in my little fire pit in our backyard. It was in the middle of the summer, and we created a campfire. I had written down all the negativity. Statements like *I will never be successful. I am a fraud. I am not worthy. I am not confident. I am dumb. I am fat.* You know, ALL the things.

I filled up multiple sheets of paper and, I am not ashamed to say, I cried while doing it. But then I watched it burn. Watching it all disappear, I felt lighter. Happier. More myself than I had in a long time. And the very next day, I closed a 5-figure client.

Can I guarantee that timetable for you?

No.

But can I guarantee that if you get rid of the head trash, you will have more room for a positive mindset and that will lead you to a more successful life?

Yes, yes, I can.

The great thing about these six pillars of a positive mindset, of unstoppable success is that they are completely up to you. You are not waiting on someone else to email you back. You are not needing to get anyone's permission to move forward. These pillars are yours. You can take action today. You can start the journey to reclaiming yourself.

This is your life. It is time that you really LIVE it.

#alwaysbetheshark,
Stevie Dawn

LIST OF STRATEGIES

- Strategy #1 Picture Your Ideal Life
- Strategy #2 Write Down Questions
- Strategy #3 Create a Vision Checklist
- Strategy #4 Examine Your Vision
- Strategy #5 Make Your Vision Stick With Your List
- Strategy #6 Retitle Yourself
- Strategy #7 Adopt the Success Model (BEBO)
- Strategy #8 Shine a Light on Your Beliefs
- Strategy #9 Tracking Your Emotions for the Win
- Strategy #10 Investigate your Habits
- Strategy #11 Tell Me What You Want, What You Really Really Want
- Strategy #12 Rewrite Beliefs That Aren't Working
- Strategy #13 Practice Before You Speak
- Strategy #14 Prep for Outcome Success
- Strategy #15 Record Your Proof of Success
- Strategy #16 Master Your Mantra
- Strategy #17 Picture Your Peeps
- Strategy #18 Fix Your Face
- Strategy #19 Bring Your Body Language to Attention

- Strategy #20 Pump Up Your Playlist!
- Strategy #21 Discover Your Place of Joy
- Strategy #22 Practice Out Loud
- Strategy #23 Make Your Highlight Reel
- Strategy #24 Remember, You Are An Expert
- Strategy #25 Practice Resilience
- Strategy #26 Identify Reality from Perception
- Strategy #27 It. Is. Totally. Okay. To. Feel. Sad
- Strategy #28 Embrace Self-Compassion
- Strategy #29 Write Your Own Permission Slip
- Strategy #30 Define Success For Yourself
- Strategy #31 Track Each Step of Your Journey
- Strategy #32 Ask Yourself a Bazillion Questions
- Strategy #33 "Paint Your Own Picture"
- Strategy #34 Know Your Habits
- Strategy #35 Like Ross, Learn How to Pivot
- Strategy #36 Recognize the Red Convertible of Opportunity
- Strategy #37 Look Fear Directly in the Eyes
- Strategy #38 Remove Attachment to the Outcome Strategy
- Strategy #39 Make a Decision
- Strategy #40 DO IT NOW!
- Strategy #41 Understand Your Brain
- Strategy #42 Write Your Own Story
- Strategy #43 Stop If/Then Living
- Strategy #44 Get Into Your Own "Shark Cage"
- Strategy #45 Define Your Habits
- Strategy #46 Identify Your Triggers
- Strategy #47 Break Up With a Habit
- Strategy #48 Turn Down the Friction
- Strategy #49 Take Messy Action
- Strategy #50 Take Out Your "Head Trash"

ABOUT THE AUTHOR

As a motivational speaker and coach, Dr. Stevie Dawn is focused on helping people to unleash unstoppable success in their lives both personally and professionally. Her experience as a 4-time business owner, along with her work in the private and public sector, allows her to enhance her presentations with real life stories and examples that are applicable to every audience.

Her educational background includes a master's degree in sociology from Wichita State University and a doctorate in leadership from Colorado State University. With over 20 years of teaching and training experience, Dr. Stevie Dawn approaches every engagement with humor, inspiration, and energy to get people moving towards their best lives.

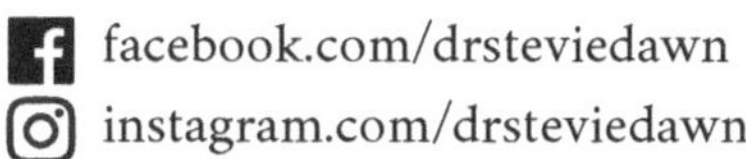

REFERENCES

Introduction

Jingle Jangle: A Christmas Journey. Directed by David E. Talbert. Netflix, 2020.

Chapter 2 The Cycles of Life

Wise, Robert, dir. *The Sound of Music*. Los Angeles. 20th Century Fox, 1965.

"What is the Self Coaching Model?" Last modified 2021. https://thelifecoachschool.com/self-coaching-model-guide/

ASPCA is the trademark of American Society For The Prevention of Cruelty To Animals, The.

Diet Coke is the trademark of Coca Cola Company, The.

Spice Girls, "Wannabe," 1996, CD Single. Virgin Records, compact disc.

REFERENCES

Chapter 3 The Six Pillars of Unstoppable Success

Jingle Jangle: A Christmas Journey. Directed by David E. Talbert. Netflix, 2020.

Chapter 4 Bold Confidence

Target is a trademark of <u>Target Brands, Inc.</u>

Marine Corps is a trademark of <u>U.S. Marine Corps, a component of the U.S. Department of the Navy.</u>

House of Pain, "Jump Around," Recorded November 1991 – May 1992. Track 2 on *House of Pain.* Tommy Boy, May 5, 1992, compact disc.

Instagram is a trademark of <u>Instagram, LLC.</u>

"Greatest Love of All," written by Linda Creed and Michael Masser, performed by Whitney Houston. Recorded 1983–1984. Track 9 on *Whitney Houston.* Arista, February 14, 1985, compact disc.

Chapter 5 Emotional Resilience and Success

Rocky. Directed by John G. Avildsen, written by Sylvester Stallone. United Artists, 1976.

Finding Nemo. Directed and written by Andrew Stanton.Walt Disney Pictures and Pixar Animation Studios. Buena Vista Pictures Distribution, 2003.

Goh, J., Pfeffer, J., & Zenios, S. A. (2015). The relationship between workplace stressors and mortality and health costs in the United States. Management Science, 62(2), 608-628.

Chapter 6 Captivating Visions—More Specific Vision

"Square Root of Possible" from *Jingle Jangle: A Christmas Journey*. Directed by David E. Talbert. Netflix, 2020.

FRIENDS. "The One with The Cop," Season 5, episode 16. Warner Brothers Television Distribution, February 25, 1999.

Chapter 8 Magnetic Mindset

Henry Ford quote, https://quoteinvestigator.com/2015/02/03/you-can/.

Chevy Malibu is a trademark of GENERAL MOTORS LLC.

Miranda, Lin-Manuel. "Hamilton: An American Musical." In *Hamilton: The Revolution*. Edited by Jeremy McCarter. New York: Grand Central Publishing, 2016.

Rowling, J. K. 2014. *Harry Potter and the Chamber of Secrets*. New York, NY: Bloomsbury Childrens Books.

Jaws. Directed by Steven Spielberg. Universal Pictures, 1975.

Shark Week is a trademark of DISCOVERY COMMUNICATIONS, LLC.

Chapter 9 Elevated Habits

"Excellence is a Habit: 7 Lessons from this Aristotle Quote," Develop Good Habits. October 29, 2020. https://www.developgoodhabits.com/excellence-habit/

CrossFit is a trademark of CROSSFIT, LLC.

REFERENCES

The Hobbit: The Motion Picture Trilogy. Directed by Peter Jackson. Warner Brothers Pictures, 2012-2014.

The Lord of the Rings. Directed by Peter Jackson. New Line Cinema, 2001-2003.

NOTES

CHAPTER 5

1. https://www.everydayhealth.com/wellness/united-states-of-stress/
2. https://workplacementalhealth.org/Mental-Health-Topics/Workplace-Stress
3. https://www.ncbi.nlm.nih.gov/pmc/articles/PMC2729718/

CHAPTER 8

1. https://www.sermoncentral.com/sermon-illustrations/64478/a-farmer-had-a-neighbor-that-was-just-absolutely-by-sherm-nichols

CHAPTER 9

1. https://dornsife.usc.edu/news/stories/3143/how-to-keep-your-new-years-resolution/
2. https://academic.oup.com/jpubhealth/article/43/2/392/5637580